PRACTICING
LIBERATION

Transformative Strategies
for Collective Healing and
Systems Change

PRACTICING
LIBERATION

EDITED BY TESSA HICKS PETERSON AND HALA KHOURI

WITH CONTRIBUTIONS FROM JACOBY BALLARD, LESLIE BOOKER,
TAJ JAMES, KERRI KELLY, SARÁ KING, NKEM NDEFO, KEELY NGUYỄN,
DALIA PARIS-SAPER, CLAUDIA VANESSA REYES, VALORIE THOMAS,
THERESE JULIA UY, AND DAVION "ZI" ZIERE

FOREWORD BY KAZU HAGA

North Atlantic Books
Huichin, unceded Ohlone land
Berkeley, California

Published by
North Atlantic Books
Huichin, unceded Ohlone land
Berkeley, California

Cover art and design by Amanda Weiss
Book design by Happenstance Type-O-Rama

Printed in Canada

Practicing Liberation: Transformative Strategies for Collective Healing and Systems Change is sponsored and published by North Atlantic Books, an educational nonprofit based in the unceded Ohlone land Huichin (Berkeley, CA) that collaborates with partners to develop cross-cultural perspectives; nurture holistic views of art, science, the humanities, and healing; and seed personal and global transformation by publishing work on the relationship of body, spirit, and nature.

North Atlantic Books's publications are distributed to the US trade and internationally by Penguin Random House Publisher Services. For further information, visit our website at www.northatlanticbooks.com.

Library of Congress Cataloging-in-Publication Data

Names: Peterson, Tessa Hicks, editor. | Khouri, Hala, editor.
Title: Practicing liberation : transformative strategies for collective
  healing and systems change / edited by Tessa Hicks Peterson and Hala
  Khouri.
Description: Berkeley, CA : North Atlantic Books, [2024] | Includes
  bibliographical references and index.
Identifiers: LCCN 2023050114 (print) | LCCN 2023050115 (ebook) | ISBN
  9798889840664 (trade paperback) | ISBN 9798889840671 (ebook)
Subjects: LCSH: Social justice. | Social change. | Community development. |
  Psychic trauma. | Healing—Social aspects.
Classification: LCC HM671 .P744 2024 (print) | LCC HM671 (ebook) | DDC
  303.3/72—dc23/eng/20231106
LC record available at https://lccn.loc.gov/2023050114
LC ebook record available at https://lccn.loc.gov/2023050115

1 2 3 4 5 6 7 8 9 MARQUIS 28 27 26 25 24

This book includes recycled material and material from well-managed forests. North Atlantic Books is committed to the protection of our environment. We print on recycled paper whenever possible and partner with printers who strive to use environmentally responsible practices.

This book is dedicated to those we are most intimately accountable to: our beloved blood and chosen families, our ancestors, known and unknown, and our future descendants. It is also dedicated to the many young people, elders, community organizers, artists, healers, colleagues, comrades, and collaborators we have been blessed to work with in our communities. We are grateful to all those who have generously shared their wisdom and practices of liberation with us and to those who have asked us to pay it forward. This is for you (and you, and you . . .).

Contents

Acknowledgments

This anthology and the *Practicing Liberation Workbook* that accompanies it draw greatly from the work of so many. The influences are far and wide, from academic scholars in psychology, sociology, organizational development, neuroscience, critical theory, and ethnic studies to the elders, youth, and mentors from spiritual traditions, organizations, and movement spaces we have been a part of. We are grateful to bring practices to these pages that we have learned in many spaces, over many decades, and hope that we have honored them well. We are cognizant in particular of the work of so many activists, healers, and social justice comrades that cultivate the movement of healing justice, which is a blessing to our generation.

We also acknowledge the diverse ancestors of our writing collective and hope we are doing justice to their dreams of the future. Likewise, we hope to do justice to our future descendants, who desperately need us to practice liberation, community care, and healing justice now so that they may have a thriving future to be born into. We recognize our accountability to them both, as well as to the earth and the Indigenous communities who seeded original restorative practices and community care long before this country was colonized. Further, we respectfully acknowledge and are indebted to the labor of the multitudes who have been forced onto this land and continue to work in the shadows for our collective benefit; this includes enslaved people and refugee- and immigrant-settlers, many of whom have been coerced to this country by militarism, imperialism, and displacement. We also understand that acknowledgment alone is insufficient to address and begin to repair the historic and ongoing harm caused by colonialism, white supremacy, and centuries of attempted genocide. We hope this work plays one small part in the larger work of reparations and community care by way of gifting back knowledges that advance healing justice to more and more of us who inhabit this fragile planet, as well as gifting back actual dollars from the residuals of this book toward funds for Indigenous rematriation.

Foreword

Kazu Haga

When I first began to get involved in the work of social change, I took words like *peace* and *justice* for granted. Like most people, I simply thought justice meant correcting society's ills and peace meant harmony.

And they do. But at the same time, it's not that simple.

Shallow understanding of complex ideas like peace and justice also leads to a shallow understanding of how change is made. I believed that if enough people marched, blockaded intersections, and chanted loudly, then change would happen, and we would achieve peace and justice.

So, I marched. I blockaded intersections. And I chanted until my throat was sore. And, despite seeing some incremental changes take place, I did not witness the depth of transformation I felt was so necessary.

And then I met Dr. Martin Luther King Jr. I mean, I didn't *really* meet him, but I studied his teachings for the first time. Ten years into my career as an activist, I began to finally understand the real Dr. King: the radical, love-fueled, anticapitalist revolutionary that society had hid from me in plain sight. And then, finally, I began to understand.

I began to understand that my idea of peace had been diluted by our society's propensity for what Dr. King called negative peace, a cheap veil of "quiet and calm" that comes at the expense of justice. He taught me that real peace, positive peace, "is not merely the absence of some negative force—war, tensions, confusion, but it is the presence of some positive force—justice, goodwill, the power of the kingdom of God."[1]

After my years of chanting "no justice, no peace!" Dr. King finally taught me what those words truly meant. Without fighting for justice in an unjust world, we will never have real, lasting, *positive* peace.

I realized that the work of peacemaking is a loud, messy, and chaotic process. I realized that we cannot be afraid to disturb negative peace, complacency, and business as usual.

But I also learned that this loud, fierce energy needs to be grounded in love.

Audre Lorde taught us that "the master's tools will never dismantle the master's house."[2] Violence is the tool of the master. Overpowering people and enforcing its will is how the empire creates change. And those changes have led to trauma, injustice, and separation.

If our goal is healing, positive peace, and reconciliation, we must find a different way to create change. We cannot force justice and enforce peace. You cannot shove healing down someone's throat.

I realized that, even in many of our social justice movements, we are grounded in a worldview of separation and leading from a place of anger and resentment. Like many activists, I had been trying to use our actions to harness power and overpower the other side. It was not that different from how the institutions I was going up against make change.

I learned that, more than anything, a commitment to building the Beloved Community that Dr. King and so many others before us fought for meant a commitment to always centering healing and reconciliation. That our goals had to be much more than legislative. They had to be about relationships.

So, I began teaching nonviolence, trying to infuse our movements with the lessons I learned from Dr. King. At the same time, I began working with incarcerated people, helping to empower the voices of those who had been most directly impacted by violence.

But after some time, I saw that even this work was only scratching the surface. I realized that even as I was encouraging activists to not see people as the enemy, there were people in my life whom I had not been able to forgive. I realized that as I was helping incarcerated people heal through the violence they had experienced, I was failing to look at my own shadows.

I realized that my healing work was focused *out there*. And I realized that my capacity to lead with love and to hold spaces for healing was limited by my own lack of healing. My understanding of interdependence would always be an intellectual one as long as there were fractures within my own body and in my own life.

I realized that I can only lead with love to the extent that I am healed. I can only work to remind us of our interdependence to the extent that I am whole.

My study of Dr. King's work taught me what it meant to chant "no justice, no peace." But my *practice* of Dr. King's teachings made me ask myself what it means to *know* justice, to *know* peace. Not just as an intellectual exercise, but to live them as an embodied practice.

From my vantage point, my personal journey seems to have run parallel to the collective journey of many changemakers. When I first started to get involved in social change work, there was no talk of healing, embodiment, or interdependence. We didn't sing, we didn't have rituals, we didn't talk about trauma.

But over the years, these words began to appear more and more in our movement's vernacular. We began to sing again. We organized rituals. We began to understand how trauma impacts *everything* we do. And we began to understand more and more that our ability to heal society's ills is directly tied to our own healing.

Right now, our movements are grappling with how to make these lessons real. How do we *embody* the change we want to see?

Being invited by this anthology's editors to participate in their Know Justice, Know Peace: A Transformation and Justice Community Collective could not have come at a better time. As global movements strive to embody the essence of peace and justice and delve deeper into the profound relationship between healing and justice, their collective work and this resulting anthology emerge as an indispensable tool for activists, healers, faith leaders, social workers, and educators alike.

The lessons that follow in these pages are an example of embodiment. Written by practitioners on the frontlines—organizers, activists, healers, educators, and faith leaders—every chapter radiates the lessons garnered from hard-fought campaigns, struggles alongside the most marginalized communities, and wisdom gleaned from deep spiritual practice.

Being an anthology fortifies this work against the pitfall of a single narrative. Within its pages, the vast diversity of the writers and their experiences serves as a powerful reminder of the necessity of a movement ecosystem as diverse as a lush rainforest.

In one chapter, you will delve into the core principles of how trauma impacts both individuals and movements, underscoring the importance of bringing in healing practices. The next chapter will drop you off right onto the frontlines of organizing, where a poignant personal account will shed light on the history—and limitations—of trauma-informed care.

One chapter will present a tangible illustration of a new cutting-edge organizational approach, while another will deliver a contemporary adaptation of a 2,500-year-old wisdom tradition, making it applicable to today's organizing world.

One chapter will offer valuable insights on how to engage in accountability practices that are healing in our movement spaces, while others will vividly depict the depth of our socialization and the pervasive influence of violent worldviews in the spaces we inhabit. In another, you will read about a compelling real-life example of racial harm, and how one courageous organization overcame it.

All of this is beautifully held within the framework that collective healing is the path to know justice and to know peace.

Dr. Cornel West encouraged us to "never forget that justice is what love looks like in public."[3] If so, our movements for justice need to be grounded in a love so powerful that we will never lose sight of it, even in the most challenging of circumstances.

As we face a world contending with climate catastrophe, pandemics, the erosion of our democratic institutions, and a long-awaited racial reckoning, this book serves as a crucial resource that can help keep us on the path toward practicing liberation.

Introduction

Tessa Hicks Peterson

In order to create a better world, we must first imagine her into being. Without radical imagination, we are left only with what we currently know, which limits what could be. adrienne maree brown reminds us that the world that we live in now—its systems, structures, norms, and expectations—was imagined by those who came before us, but did not include all of us.[1] What can we imagine, and then create together, that would ensure that liberty and justice for all was an actual lived experience for all? What repair and healing do we need to move beyond surviving and into thriving as we build the world we want? If we do not practice those values and qualities now, in the very act of imagining and creating the just and liberating world we need, we not only set ourselves up to reproduce old harms under new leadership, but we also will not know how to take care of ourselves and each other in the new systems we create.

So, what is this world we dream of? What would it look like, feel like, and sound like there? To have our needs met. To live in peace. To matter. To belong. To be whole. To be cared for. To love and be loved. This is at the root of the world we deserve and need. And to create it, we must enact it with each other until we shift the systems we are part of to also reflect it.

Yet, most people working to create a better world suffer from traumas of injustice as well as burnout and isolation caused by hyperproductivity, hypercompetition, and hyperindividualism. As such, ideas of living day to day in peace, love, and wholeness can seem unattainable—due both to external factors that can make even survival a luxury and to internal habits that make such things seemingly inaccessible or impractical. As a result, changemakers tend to negotiate high levels of stress, health challenges, and fatigue—then often are disposed of when they burn out or slip up. In many cases, changemakers feel the need for a healthier and more whole life but are also grief-stricken by the hypocrisy of organizations or movements that do not live the values they preach. Often, changemakers feel like they have little recourse to change either. At the same time, they are carrying with them tremendous skills and practices that keep them and their movements resilient in the face of tyranny.

But, what if the tyranny of exhaustion, fragmentation, and stress are partially self-imposed and are limiting the power of our organizations, movements, and vision of the world we want? What if we could integrate new ideas, tools, and practices into our personal and collective lives that would elevate commitments to caring for ourselves and our communities and translate into more sustainable ways in which our organizations and movements could operate? What if we discovered that slowing down to take care of ourselves and each other, to invest in relationships, to put the values of community liberation and wellness into our daily work practices and structures allows us to feel better and more interconnected as we do the work of re-creating a better world? What if we created the world we want in the one we have and even felt joy, connection, and sustainability in the process of that hard work of change? What if the work itself felt life-giving and restorative rather than draining and conflictual?

The scholar-activists and practitioners who have come together to write this book aim to imagine into being these very things. Through their many years of study and practice, they share knowledge, models, and stories that introduce new and very ancient ways of caring for ourselves and our communities. They also share reflections, strategies, and practices to advance radical social change not only at a systems level but also in how we live our way into the new kinds of systems we are imagining. Igniting the power of imagination and creation, these writers explore new ways of understanding our problems and our solutions—and ourselves, in the process. They speak to healing and justice as decolonial, heart-centered, trauma-informed, embodied practices. They also break down what that means and how to operationalize it in real-time—from guiding principles to collective governance, from self-realization to organizational development, from collective healing to critical consciousness raising. They speak of neurophysiology and trauma, of Dharma and embodiment, of Indigenous knowledge and healing justice and provide tangible practices that lead to personal and structural transformation. They write as and to community organizers and activists, teachers and healers, service providers and organizational leaders. And they invite you to join them in collectively imagining a better world into being—and practicing it together, here and now.

Framework

Radical feminist organizers and scholar-activists have long emphasized the importance of connecting social justice activism to radical healing practices—not only as strategies for change, but of survival.[2] Indigenous communities and ancient wisdom traditions throughout the world have long espoused values of interconnectedness of mind, body, spirit and of individuals, communities, and ecosystems. The models for regenerative and restorative practices that we desperately need today are as old as— and directly connected to—our impulse to repair the world. Thus, what we need is the very knowledge that we hold in our bones, in our ancestral memories, in histories both abandoned and stolen. This book is a vehicle for re-membering—that is, bringing the members of such knowing and communal practicing back together, with the added value of what new science, consciousness, and traditions can bring to a (re)mix that will deepen and expand strategies to sustain ourselves in the world we live in today.

Calls for such re-membering and emergent strategies have grown even more strongly in recent years, in circles of frontline organizers, healers, and scholars desiring more transformative practices to sustain themselves and their movements.[3] *Healing justice* emerged within the last twenty years as a powerful collective care movement to address generational trauma and oppression and radically reimagine collective care, safety, accountability, and healing as part of liberatory political strategy and practice. This framework emerged formally in 2006 through Kindred Southern Healing Justice Collective, alongside other directly impacted feminist activists and healers who survive trauma and oppression by drawing on embodied liberatory practices.[4] Healing justice recognizes the need for social movements to weave together ancestral wisdom traditions of healing and knowledge around community care and repair with critical imaginings of change that do not reproduce systemic-isms and interpersonal harm. With strong roots in anticapitalism, abolition, and Black feminism, this framework is integral to paradigm shifts in organizations and communities yearning for more roadmaps that are justice oriented, healing centered, and community led.

Rather than suppressing individualized symptoms of trauma, the process of healing justice is asset driven, engaging in our cultural identities and lived experiences "to regenerate traditions that have been lost; to mindfully hold contradictions in our practices; and to be conscious of the conditions we are living and working inside of as healers and organizers in our communities and movements."[5] Healing justice advances addressing the root causes of trauma and responses to harm centered on resilience, wholeness, and wellness as a mode of organizing and movement work. As echoed by organizer Tanuja Jagernauth, "we have bodies, minds, emotions, hearts, and it makes the connection that we cannot do this work of transforming society and our communities without bringing collective healing into our work."[6] This healing work is political by engaging in practices to decolonize the mind against colonialism and white supremacy and reclaim individual bodies, spirits, and histories that have been violently erased by hegemonic forces. By disrupting the pervasive nature of violence and harm on a local level, radical care for the self and community expands the capacity of collectives to practice an ideal vision of the future outside of dominant paradigms. Shifting from norms of domination and extraction to those of interconnection and regeneration will require infrastructures and practices that align with collectively held values and futures.

Book Overview

The formation of this anthology arose out of deep longing to better understand for ourselves and share with others the multiple ways social services and social movements can transform how to work for well-being and justice with greater sustainability, integrity, joy, and bold vision. We have worked for decades toward this kind of transformation and have been moved by the unique ways so many of our admired comrades and colleagues have "lived the questions" of this journey for healing and justice. We are grateful that they enthusiastically accepted our invitation to map these ways into words and visions to be shared with all of you.

Authors in this anthology are connected to a cross section of locations and movements; we believe our experiences might resonate with or inspire anyone who seeks to create change and transformation, particularly those who work for justice, health, wellness, community building, education, arts, and healing work—including service providers, educators, health professionals, community organizers, and people working at community foundations and nonprofit and grassroots organizations. Authors use language that most directly relates to their field and experience, some of which may align and resonate with you and some of which may introduce unfamiliar terms or ideas. We make no attempt to make these offerings uniform but rather celebrate the diversity of voices and life experiences that come to bear on the phenomena explored in this book.

This book invites us to align liberatory values with how we, and our organizations, operate in daily life. This work is grounded in the realities of the traumas of injustice—targeted oppression, violence, corruption, and unjust attacks on our communities. It looks these squarely in the eye and does not offer a single prescription for their dismantling; rather, it offers a clear analysis of their formation and tangible, life-giving strategies for building critical resilience and joy alongside our resistance and work for change. Our guiding principles include an understanding of the long-lasting and intergenerational stress that can result from trauma and injustice as well as the diverse forms of healing and transformative tools we can use to practice liberation as both a means and an end.

We underscore here what it can look like to occupy the liminal space of *practicing liberation*. Even those who think they are free because they benefit from these systems are locked in systems of oppression that diminish the humanity of all involved. As our foremothers have shared in movements over time, "until we are all free, we are none of us free."[7] Here we practice how to get free together in our daily work, in our own bodies, in our communities, and in the organizations and systems we are reinventing, reimagining, and rebuilding. Through different entry ways and with different focal points, these diverse authors bring from theory to practice transformative strategies for collective healing and systems change.

There is an arc to the way we ordered this collection, which unfolds through three main sections: *Frameworks* (distinct but connected lenses offered to explore personal and systems change); *Practices* (embodied concepts for critical self-awareness, community accountability, and deep transformation); and *Liberatory Futures* (intimate, fugitive explorations of how to transmute harm into repair and shift old organizing tactics toward transformative healing). The book begins with an overview of common challenges confronted by changemakers and strategies used to address them (Chapter 1). This is followed by more examples from organizational leaders who share frameworks for trauma- and healing-informed resilience, systemic transformation, and collective emergence that can be operationalized at organizational levels (Chapters 2 and 3). The second section (Chapters 4, 5, and 6) then hones in on more nuanced practices for changemakers to deepen their critical consciousness and commitments to accountability, compassion, and liberation at individual and community levels. Chapters 7 and 8 begin the last section by sharing intimate narratives of confronting suffering inside organizations due to ingrained toxic norms and how the authors went about cultivating both resistance and resilience to survive and for healing-in-action practices to thrive.

The closing chapter brings the possibility of liberatory futures into sharper focus by way of exploring frameworks and stories of transformative movement organizing within Beloved Communities. This arc makes sense to us, but you may wish to dive in from another entry point. Our aim is to provide less of a roadmap and more of a North Star. Through different practices, theories of change, and stories of meaningful transformation, we hope this book provides support for cultivating what healing and liberation can look like both within our bodies and communities and inside of (and despite) existing dominant systems. For even more tangible and readily applicable practices for individuals and organizations, we also invite readers to read the accompanying workbook, *Practicing Liberation Workbook: Radical Tools for Grassroots Activists, Community Leaders, Teachers, and Caretakers Working toward Social Justice.*

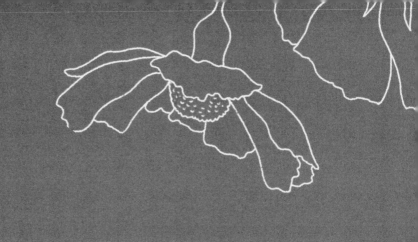

FRAMEWORKS

1

KNOW JUSTICE, KNOW PEACE

Insights from a Transformation and Justice Community Collective

Tessa Hicks Peterson, Keely Nguyễn, Dalia Paris-Saper,
Claudia Vanessa Reyes, and Therese Julia Uy

Working toward well-being and liberation amid the myriad global crises that exist is some of the most critical work we can do today.[1] Luckily, many organizations are working to heal the wounds of violence and systemic inequities and to create cultural shifts toward community care and social justice. Yet even the most well-intended social change efforts can be overcome by stress, exhaustion, interpersonal conflict, and general disillusionment with the way community justice and well-being ideals often fall short in practice.

The authors of this chapter have each been a part of and witnessed the fruits of healing justice practice as well as the challenges of community change efforts. Collectively, we felt a calling for societal transformation rooted in a love ethic—a shared commitment to personal and collective change grounded in radical care.[2] We knew that we were not alone in these longings and struggles and came together to cocreate a community-based, participatory action research project called Know Justice, Know Peace: A Transformation and Justice Community Collective in collaboration with community changemakers from six grassroots social justice–oriented organizations.[3] This collective engaged in conversations, interviews, surveys, and healing circles with staff and leadership at partner organizations to identify needs, barriers, and facilitators of actualizing healing, well-being, and justice values in daily operation, strategic vision, and organizational governance. In response to what we learned in that process, we created an eight-month, biweekly training program to explore frameworks, strategies, and practices to address these issues. Overall, we found what leading activist-scholars have also increasingly identified— that in order to be effective in our work, and to thrive individually and organizationally in spite of the oppressive realities that exist, we must transform the relationships and structures we operate in so we can embody the values that promote collective care and disrupt those that don't.[4]

Members of our collective responded enthusiastically to the conversations we had about these topics and the series of trainings and workshops we engaged in on issues of trauma-informed care, transformative movement organizing, nonviolence philosophy, and embodied healing practices from a variety of traditions. They shared that integrating healing justice practices and frameworks in their daily life, political strategy, and organizational structure were critical for the future of their communities and their own lives. They also voiced how very hard it is to sustain this in social change work faced with threats of violence, burnout, and organizational conflict. They shared the emotional weight of the traumas of injustice that they and their communities have experienced and how paradigms of hyperproductivity, urgency, and competition often thwart practices that align values for collective care in organizational culture. They spoke of wanting more tools to stay grounded and connected while advancing effective strategies to resist toxic structures and replace them with transformative ones. They desired to learn (and re-member) intentional practices to sustain themselves, the communities they work with, and their own organizational culture, seeing individual well-being as connected to collective well-being and social change.

Realizing the need to level up the impact of this work, we invited several of the guest practitioners from our eight-month training program, and others whose work aligned with these goals, to expand on these concepts and their applications in writing.[5] This anthology is the result. We hope it responds directly to the call we received from those on the frontlines to explore diverse and ever-deepening ways to center liberation, collective care, and restorative practices in the work of organizational development and social justice.

What follows in this opening chapter is a summary of what we learned in our collective's action research and training together about the things changemakers struggle with as well as the assets they build upon, the areas where they want to integrate new ideas and practices, and the tools they already use for their own surviving and thriving. We have organized an exploration of these topics into three main areas— surviving on the frontlines of systemic injustice, community care, and organizational culture shift—that we hope will resonate with others experiencing similar phenomena. Although the individuals in our collective primarily identify as community organizers, activists, or staff members of grassroots organizations, we use the umbrella term *change-makers* throughout this chapter as we believe this term encompasses both this constituency and those who may be inclined to read this book. We see everyone in education and community mental health as change-makers, as well as people who are engaged in any efforts to address suffering, transform power, and uplift humanity.

Surviving on the Frontlines of Systemic Injustice

Most people would agree that living and working in ways that embody well-being, peace, and justice would be great, but there are many very real individual and systemic challenges and threats to doing so. When someone's social change work is rooted in their own personal experiences of injustice or violence or ones that directly affect communities they are a part of, they are more vulnerable to the pain triggered by exposure to direct and vicarious sources of trauma and marginalization. Some who are drawn to changemaking work have privileges that provide greater buffers or support systems with which to negotiate vicarious trauma, while other individuals who have fewer buffers from direct impact by inequity, oppression, or historical trauma may face more frequent and intense impacts of vicarious trauma or burnout.[6] Healing direct or vicarious trauma requires great vulnerability, fortitude, and emotional labor and is best supported by skillful facilitation, tools, and practices to navigate the discomfort and move toward authentic healing. A certain level of discomfort occurs in the healing of unhealthy personal and familial histories as well as when experiencing the repercussions of systemic suffering. The hope is that by confronting such discomfort, changemakers acquire greater tools for negotiating and lessening the resulting suffering.

The changemakers in our collective emphasized the need for such trauma-informed, healing-centered knowledge, tools, and facilitation skills to process the trauma that occurs as a result of their work. Nearly half of our collective indicated that the work they do can bring up past trauma, and many found that the emotional impact of their work is their primary stressor. Trauma-informed healing practices can not only guide members through their own healing but also aid in the healing of those that they lead/teach/serve/organize.

In conditions in which the sociopolitical stakes are high, funding is low, and hyperproductivity is the norm, feeling stressed at work or over work-related matters occurs with greater regularity and force. Given their physical and emotional investment in the cause they care about and work for, changemakers in our collective felt particularly susceptible to work-related stress, especially those who are working in their own community or who are confronted by familiar distressing conditions. Interestingly, when we did activities to reflect on our states of stress, many found a differentiation between how much stress they confront in work and how much stress they *feel* from it, indicating that many feel more stress than they actually confront. Others found that they feel little stress, even though great stressors exist. Members found that becoming aware of the differentiation between the stress that exists and its impact has helped them assess the effectiveness of their stress management skills. As such, they also voiced a need for more self-awareness and stress-reduction practices that would help them identify, cope with, and negotiate the stress present in their lives and how it lands in their minds, bodies, and spirits on a daily basis.

Changemakers find that much of social change work involves the added pressure of constantly being exposed to distressing incidents via direct contact, graphics, cases, and social media, which can exacerbate primary and secondary traumatic stress levels and trigger personal and vicarious forms of trauma.[7] When illustrating the daily scope of such exposure, a member of our collective (who works in a network for detention and deportation rapid response) shared their experience of being triggered by such direct engagement: "I'm the one who gets the phone calls . . . [and reviews the voicemail] recordings. I couldn't even listen to the graphic details of the recordings because I just don't want to relive it . . . and then we just had a campaign and the images—they're just so real."

In the age of digital technology and social media, it is challenging for changemakers to find a balance. They cannot escape a wide range of injustices that are broadcasted throughout the world, in addition to the ones they have direct contact with. Such exposure to distressing events and vicarious trauma can tamper with their well-being and lead to burnout symptoms; yet being frontline recipients of stories of direct suffering and staying up to date on current events related to the organization's work are often expectations of the job. Being proximate to and advocating on behalf of deep human suffering without it taking over one's whole being requires a level of attuned presence and skill that many felt they needed more support for.

The nature of social justice work and/or media consumption today is that both often feel simultaneously urgent, necessary, and stressful. Members in our collective discussed that the urgency they felt about the work exists because their own lives, or the lives of their loved ones, often depend on it. However, while urgency can be a factor leading to high stress, it is also a major mobilizing force behind grassroots activism that empowers people to advocate for their own rights, well-being, and justice. A kind of powerful organizing comes out of this urgency, a mobilization built on the faith and need to win a struggle for equity or rights, a motivation that defies despair and hopelessness. One member shared that "the power I feel we are creating motivates me." Another said that when they feel overwhelmed, "the community we are fighting for motivates me to keep going. We have to keep going for them and those who follow." Many negotiate daily tension between motivation and exhaustion resulting from this sense of urgency.

In our deepening explorations of stress, we discussed the stress that results from urgent obligations and deadlines and extends into excess stress that comes from unresolved trauma (one's own or that of others one works with). One member stated, "I worry about other people's lives . . . We deal with a lot of misery; we deal with a lot of grief . . . It's stressful." Many communicated that the stress of colleagues and community members impacted their energy and emotions and, that on top of personal life stressors, chronic burnout symptoms increased. Feelings of exhaustion, fatigue, isolation, irritability, lack of productivity, defeat, and being overwhelmed were frequent conditions experienced by changemakers. An organizer working in a grassroots justice organization shared: "Our sleep is not consistent . . . work is on our mind all the time."

Changemakers also often extend their availability past work hours to support individuals who seek their help. A community organizer working for carceral justice recalled receiving text messages at ten o'clock at night from someone she didn't know, asking for her help. Caring deeply and being closely connected to community members who experience emotional pain, this organizer emphasized

> *I don't want them to feel like they're alone. Like I was alone once . . .*
> *so that stresses me a lot. I can't help but to feel, like, I've been there, I*
> *know what they're going through. I know what it feels like not to have*
> *no one to turn to or not to understand something. So sometimes it's just,*
> *you know, with them calling late night or texting at night or calling me*
> *crying, I remember. There were times I called people myself. I still*
> *cry today.*

Most individuals who choose to do this kind of work are not working in a typical nine-to-five job where you can arrive home and separate yourself from work until the next day. Since most changemakers' work is tied to personal identities in some way, many carry deep feelings of responsibility to support their communities. Dedication to social change makes it difficult to maintain boundaries between professional and home life, as professional identity is often interwoven with personal identity. As changemakers, we are often interdependent parts of the communities we serve, and our experiences of oppression are interconnected with those of the community members we work with. Fragmenting personal and professional life is a Western-imposed binary that does not always resonate with those whose community and work are one and the same. Dominant Western cultural norms that tie productivity to worth, that value the individual over the collective, and that fragment personal and professional spheres can lead to overwork, perfectionism, burnout, and isolation.

Many are also influenced by the culture of selflessness and martyrdom typical in changemaking communities and institutions. Some are motivated by changemaking community cultural norms that prioritize the well-being of the collective over the individual. One changemaker agreed with the usefulness of mental health days offered by their organization but refused to take them because of their fear that doing so might negatively impact their community or that they might be judged for taking a day off. Due to their strong sense of belonging and obligation to their communities, changemakers can feel guilt or even shame for taking time off. Selflessness and willingness to sacrifice their time to support their community can prevent changemakers from prioritizing their own well-being; many indicated that self-care is a selfish act. It was also mentioned repeatedly that self-care was thought of as therapy and spa treatments—something either not prioritized or inaccessible, in both time and money, for many.

This kind of work would not exist, thrive, or be able to create meaningful change without people acting out of urgency, love, and desire for justice. The more complicated task, however, is to understand where exactly stress management and self-care fit within this urgency. This requires discerning in what ways and when slowing down and attending to self-care might enable better negotiation of an urgent issue at hand and in what ways and when they would detract from it. Overall, our collective recognized we needed to uplift rest and well-being but often found it difficult to prioritize well-being practices when faced with a culture of urgency. One member spoke about the valid need for stress reduction practices but problematized these practices when they felt like the practices were a barrier to doing their community work:

> If I take a day off, if I have a mental health day, who's gonna pick up the phone if something happens to someone, you know? Who's going to be that form of communication? So, it's not that I don't want to. Of course, I do. But it's also the responsibility of not myself, but of the people inside the detention center since I'm their form of communication from the outside world.

While this quote references one individual who works in immigrant justice, most social change organizations require constant communication with community members, and most feel a sense of urgent responsibility to be there when needed. Similarly, workplace structures may allow employees to take time off, but if their responsibilities aren't covered, staff can fall behind in their work, which causes more stress for them in the end. Whatever care practices are incorporated into organizational daily life must be done thoughtfully, and with shifts covered, so that employees can operate within realistic workloads and frequent emergency situations. This next section explores care practices individuals, communities, and organizations can implement to tangibly offer solutions that directly address this and other tensions explored thus far.

Community Care

Most community organizations are founded to provide basic resources, to protect against threats of violence or injustice, and to advance the rights, wellbeing, and dignity of marginalized communities. Many organizations have arisen as acts of resistance to unjust dynamics and as acts of affirmation that community-led knowledge and power can create the equity and justice needed. The organizations in our collective were originally created to actualize change through local cultural capital, power, and knowledge. Organizing around a shared problem and set of values allows changemakers to reimagine and embody the possibilities of a future brought about by social movement. As one member of our collective stated, "The systems are inherently unjust, the systems are inherently biased, the systems are inherently disempowering. So, I think [my organization] is quite the opposite. It's very empowering. And I think that everybody is encouraged to bring their 'A Game.'" When the changemakers in this collective saw their organizations as catalysts for change, it encouraged them to show up as their whole and best selves.

Most members of our collective felt that their community organizations do their best to ensure that changemakers are acknowledged and cared for through their hard work. One organizer stated, "I love being here. [My organization] has very much been an oasis in my career, in organizing, for positivity and mutual support. You know, we've intentionally

19

tried to embody that in the program we're creating." When our well-being suffers daily due to the realities of oppression, individual and collective practices of care are a critical form of resistance, resilience, and rebuttal. It is critical that the power of (re)establishing well-being is in the hands of the person whose well-being is being threatened. This provides refueling, grounding, and self-love for those who may otherwise be undergoing a debilitating state of structural or personal violence. Given the sense of scarcity and urgency that undergird most nonprofit organizations working for justice, it is no small feat that many of these changemakers felt that their organizations do their best to engage in community care practices.

Part of the essence of community care that these changemakers reported experiencing included being able to work with like-minded, passionate people who contribute to the goal of meaningfully supporting each other, their communities, and their causes. Given that most individuals hold at least one marginalized identity in the dominant culture (that is, being queer, undocumented, formerly incarcerated, disabled, etc.), finding a home in communities of shared identities and justice values provides a deep sense of purpose and belonging—qualities that fuel a sense of safety and power amid fights against injustice. Changemakers often feel sustained by the work as a result. As one member said, "Our team has a really great support system . . . just there to help or guide, give advice, or even just to talk to." The care and love members of our collective give to one another was apparent in how they spoke together through challenging topics in our gatherings, in the way that they continue to show up each day to advocate for their communities, and in the sense of unity through their work.

Changemakers also voiced a deep sense of belonging, emotional connection, and accountability to the larger social movements they are a part of. They made it clear that their organizations place an emphasis on working directly with and being led by systems-impacted communities, placing this at the heart of their work. As mentioned, these changemakers are often a part of the communities they serve, fighting for issues that directly impact them and their families, and as a result, their own well-being and visions for justice are intertwined with those of the community. These changemakers' dedication to their communities and to collective well-being guides the work that they do toward liberation and justice.

Not all readers may resonate with the experience of working in organizations that resemble their communities, provide worker support, or inspire passion and joy. Others may find that organizations they are a part of disregard local knowledge and assets and sweep in to "help the needy" in ways that are patronizing, or deficit based. Certainly, organizations of all types exist along the continuums that exist in nonprofit and education systems. But even in our collective, where most reported they felt at home in and cared for by their organizations, there were many identifiable ways to strengthen community care and empowerment among workers. One suggestion that came up repeatedly in our collective was to support and prioritize community building among organization members. This allows for building trust, strengthening relationships, and fostering belonging, which are all key to feeling valued, taken care of, and whole. Work for justice rests squarely on a deeply connected community; as Rev. Jen Bailey reminds us: "Relationships are built at the speed of trust, and social change happens at the speed of relationships."[8]

Members noted that organizations could uplift well-being further in the work by "[spending] more time together in non-workspaces as an organization. Bonding and growing together in ways that do not involve work. Checking in with each other and setting schedules to rotate who checks in on who." Another communicated the need for leadership to "remind us that it's okay to take breaks. Check in on us. [Do] group activities as a team, not related to work." By increasing interactions on a personal level, organizations can begin to support community building within the organizations themselves. By building that from the inside, changemakers are able to connect in ways that are personal, communal, and healing. Not only does community building and connection directly fortify well-being and sense of belonging, but it also strengthens the bonds internally so that changemakers are better situated to navigate conflict and stress when they arise, which is another way to maintain community care in the face of urgent and heavy work.

In addition to taking time to check in with each other, changemakers also voiced a desire to spend more time learning and dedicating themselves to healing practices that could be integrated into their lives, communities, and workspaces. They felt that this was something important to do; however, some were unsure of how to do it. As noted, for many people drawn toward activism or the helping professions, self-care can feel selfish, indulgent, and superficial. Being able to see that caring for themselves is what allows them to do their work effectively (and even joyfully) can be one way to let go of the resistance toward these practices. In our work together, several ideas arose for simple but transformative trauma-informed, healing practices that could be brought into the workspace regularly. These included conducting breathing exercises, embodied movement practices, and other well-being activities, both individually and as a group. Such practices help changemakers to feel grounded and connected internally, interpersonally, and across communities of workers and were suggested to be integrated at the beginning of staff meetings or amid challenging decisions or disagreements. Members of our collective also suggested that organizations could facilitate routine listening circles in which changemakers could discuss their challenges or hardships in the work or share valuable practices that help them sustain themselves in the midst of it. They also suggested engaging all members of an organization in regular gatherings to embody practices together, such as grounding and mindfulness exercises, community meals, dance parties, or well-being days (self-led or facilitated by others).[9]

Our collective also explored why some methods of healing do not meet needs. For example, listening circles can be useful and validating for many, but when sharing painful narratives brings emotional distress to the surface, there is potential for trauma to be furthered, especially if there is no plan for navigating it or following up. As such, organizations that attempt to reflect with staff about traumatic occurrences that take place in their communities or movements must do so with thoughtful facilitation and must not ask members to share their traumas and then leave them to sit with all of that alone. Organizations must plan to take actions in between structured reflections; for example, after community sharing, it can be helpful to offer a simple list of steps to take when a member feels anxious, overwhelmed, or stressed. Sometimes one-on-one follow-up check-ins can help. Organizations must consider members' needs for meaningful and sustained care of their well-being so staff feel supported in work that will invariably challenge it. Ensuring that healing work around trauma is invested in as a long-term priority, not just a one-time team-bonding activity, is crucial. Training for all staff members in trauma-informed, healing-centered, and embodied strategies was brought up repeatedly as a worthy investment of the organization's time and resources as well as personal time and resources.

Our collective also underscored how important it is to keep in mind various communication styles, cultural models, or processing approaches when engaging in trauma-informed practices to make healing accessible to all. One member expressed, "It's always been a stress to even communicate how I'm feeling . . . I'm more of a writer. I like to write my feelings down versus express them to other folks." This is important to the way we understand healing, and how that is influenced by what models we have internalized to be most successful. While some may find journal writing more nurturing than talking circles, others may experience catharsis through counseling, movement, or ritual. One best practice inside of organizations is to make sure there is a variety of ways that support is offered to include the various ways people process information and feel comfortable.

Another member shared that even the act of having these conversations is difficult when she does not share close relationships with folks she is in conversation with: "It's work to even communicate how I'm really feeling because I feel like sometimes, I save those conversations for people who I've had longer relationships with and who've seen me progress and be who I am today." This statement makes it clear that strong relationships with coworkers are crucial if we are to have these difficult conversations. As we work to build those relationships, we must think about how we intentionally set the tone and create a space of support for all participating. One collective member expressed feeling comforted when people were honest and vulnerable in sharing stories because it "opens up channels" for others to share, and subsequently feel they are on the path for healing. Another suggested that "periodic healing circles would help in seeing our personal progress and give [us] opportunities to share with one another . . . remind [us] that we are all in this together." They felt that sharing these kinds of spaces helps reenergize them in their work and reinforces that they are a collective that cares about each other's well-being. Others expressed a desire to process such emotional material with friends, families, and counselors and simply wished workspaces made more room for individuals to take the time they need to process after traumatic incidents took place in their work.

Our discussions brought up additional questions collective members wanted to reflect on in order to more thoughtfully cultivate community care in their organizations, in their movements, and in their communities. These included:

- How can trauma-informed and healing-centered practices be done in a safe and sustainable way that helps members meaningfully navigate discomfort?
- How can culturally relevant and diverse approaches, traditions, and embodied modes of healing and community building be included?
- How can this be done in a communal act of resistance rather than as individualized acts of self-soothing?

- How might it look when engaging multiple approaches, such as art-based and embodied healing methods, meditation, drama, poetry, music, movement, drawing, council, communal cooking and eating, and other traditional practices of community care?

- How can healing approaches from different traditions be explored without perpetuating cultural appropriation?

- How can healing practices become accessible for all, not just integrating but prioritizing different ways of engaging in practices (e.g., those who feel the most comfortable speaking in their native language; those who struggle with expressing themselves with words; and those who are neurodivergent)?

- How can healing work move beyond cognitive and emotional expression into embodied or spiritual expression, too?

- What training, tools, knowledge, or models would support these alternative forms of expression?

- How can organizations strike a balance for healing to take place in the workplace but also ensure they prioritize members making spaces outside of work for healing so as not to overlook the reality that most personal healing can't take place in the middle of a staff meeting?

- How can organizations intentionally create the appropriate boundaries of community care that happen in the workplace so that urgent organizational goals and timelines are not usurped by personal healing work, and yet still make it so the workplace is somewhere that people can arrive as their whole selves and feel supported when the work itself triggers trauma?

- How can organizations demonstrate healing and community care in their values and actions in everything from program development, governance, conflict resolution, fiscal matters, and policies for worker engagement to general organizational culture?

These are the questions we cultivated through the research, training, and practices of our ongoing work as a collective—ones that have led us directly to the ideas and models that are focal points of this book.

Organizational Culture Shifts

While striving to embody transformative practices that align with their values and vision, members in our collective discussed structural challenges they face as part of the nonprofit industrial complex. We imagine the same may be true for educators inside of under-resourced educational systems and community health professionals who feel challenged by the bureaucracy and unrealistic expectations they may face. Myriad challenges arise when facing restrictive institutional expectations and impacts regarding funding, management hierarchies, and decision-making. A member of our collective admitted that newcomers come in with an "illusion" of their organization, and ultimately leave due to feeling "disappointed" and "deluded" that staff members did not talk about "going against oppression every day." They illustrated the realities of operating under a capitalist system, sharing that many young activists come to their organization "with a whole image of a perfect social justice organization of all their dreams," only to find that the organization is operating under the same values, organizational structures, and norms that can reproduce inequities and a lack of community care practices.

Structural implications of high turnover and reduced flexibility can result in feelings of disappointment and a culture of toxicity being replicated in the workplace. For example, one member stated:

Yesterday, I worked 11 hours. Today I am going to work more than 12 hours from when I arrive until I leave. We are all working a lot and . . . succeeding in many ways [while] barely being able to maintain it. And, then with the criticism [from other staff], we are barely able to breathe in the day.

Organizations are not immune to the pressures of neoliberalism's internalized norms of power hoarding, hyperproductivity, competition, and urgency that supersede priorities of equity, community-building, and rest. Another organizer explains:

> *I think our org, as many orgs, probably has the intention of supporting and creating space for self-care. But I think in actual practice, a lot of times we just end up replicating outside systems and end up, a lot of time, it feels like it's starting to be run like a corporation. You know, just replicating that same atmosphere of productivity, productivity, productivity; what do you do? What have you accomplished? Have you gotten this done by this time? Have you met this deadline? And look, there's obviously a lot of important things at stake that we do.*

This creates a very real tension, as the rates of violence, discrimination, and lack of support of basic needs for those most vulnerable are advancing rapidly, making it feel impossible to slow down and take care of ourselves during critical daily work. Many changemakers alluded to the sense of urgency, perfectionism, and stress in their organizations that prevent them from tending to their well-being. Some changemakers felt like they were "living by the clock" and experiencing a "time famine," a phenomenon that takes place when people are chained to the clock and become emotionally and physically depleted and dissatisfied with their lives.[11] Feeling compelled to be productive and complete tasks before deadlines, changemakers are consistently accountable to multiple constituents, including their colleagues, bosses, funders, and community members. An organizer in a leadership position candidly explained, "I don't know how to not replicate the system . . . we have to be on top of everyone's productivity," while another organizer described, "We have funders and grants to meet, we have deadlines, people to serve . . . it's almost like being a corporation where you get your certain amount of sick days or paid leave days. When that's up, you have to suck it up and get back to work." These experiences were shared among several changemakers, suggesting that deleterious cultural norms of hyperproductivity at the expense of individual and communal well-being are deeply embedded in nonprofit organizational structures.

These, of course, are also deeply embedded in dominant US culture, where ever-present messaging tells us more is better; faster is better; and we have so much to do, buy, see, learn, create that we better hustle or else we'll be left behind, lost, broke, or canceled.[10] This is not by chance. Our very economic system puts value on all entities (individuals, institutions) for what they produce (and how quickly and how much). Many Americans have been conditioned to translate economic evaluations into social and emotional ones: my worth is based on the value of what I produce. Not being valued for who you are or for simply being, but only for what you make or earn or your output, has many noxious effects.

To disrupt organizational structure, leadership, and culture that do not align with liberatory, just, and caretaking values is an enormous task, one requiring much critical reflection and accountable action. Getting to the root of the matter requires putting our attention on our most ancient national wounds that have both informed and threatened the very foundation of social, medical, political, economic, and educational systems in the US. These are the inherited systems we live with that have been shaped in their founding by such ideologies as white supremacy, racism, sexism, classism, ableism, heteronormativity, religious intolerance, and xenophobia. The results are the traumas we have inherited born of injustice, oppression, and state violence. The subsequential societal conditioning and shared traumas of these enacted ideologies have infiltrated our collective consciousness and social systems—even the ones meant to undo such harm. These are topics that members of our collective consistently spoke to and struggled with, especially as their implications showed up in their daily operations.

The repercussions of operating from systems steeped in hierarchies, competition, power hoarding, scarcity, and exclusion show up in the ways we think, feel, and operate as individuals and as groups. They come out in how power is used, understood, respected, or weaponized (in organizational governance, charitable giving, fiscal structures, leadership hierarchies, and evaluating outputs). Finally, they show up in the agreements under which we operate as a community (e.g., how we communicate, negotiate conflict, make amends, and connect as a collective). We cannot skip over or only superficially perform the systemic and personal disruptions that are needed to address these toxic norms.

Motivated by what we learned through our collective's discussions of these topics, we were moved to find frameworks that could help us reflect on how, why, and toward what end we can create meaningful culture shifts in our organizations. We found that the Three Horizons framework provides important questions that organizations can use to launch critical reflection about the systems they are operating under and what is working, what is not, and how we might facilitate an effective and generative process of change to radically transform them.[12] The questions include:

- Where do you see this system failing and how are you impacted by it?
- What toxic norms have you become conditioned to that should be questioned?
- Where do you see this system thriving and having a positive impact?
- What assets and strengths do you want to harness?
- What can you dream up that would better suit your visions of humanizing working, collaborating, serving, and leading?
- What actors are already working on this, and who can be collaborated with so the new system scales and spreads? What history, values, and culture are embedded within such new systems?
- What might a better changemaking organization or movement look, feel, and sound like?

At the heart of the work of our collective, it was clear that changemakers want to shift systemic problems at the root. Of course, the reality continues that this work of structural and systemic change is long and hard, and we must have recourse on the journey to protect ourselves from the traumas, stress, illnesses, and sorrow that result from this work *in the moment*. As such, we must both address the root causes of these conditions *and* highlight ways organizations working on these root issues can practice new or regenerate old practices to take care of workers in the process. We need to adopt care strategies that make sense amid the very real and urgent demands involved in community work *and* ones that cultivate a long-term organizational culture shift to prioritize well-being and sustainability practices.

Recognizing that if we continue to utilize the same norms and tactics that have gotten us to this place, we will likely never get out of it, our collective was eager to explore new means that might lead to new ends. Learning alternative and restorative practices for how to operate differently and still meet the increasing demands and navigate the unequal power structures they are fighting against was something many were interested in, and their desire to not replicate social inequities was clear. Executive directors, in particular, were interested in detailed strategies for policy and practice that would offer alternative structures for their organizations to grow into. Staff members also voiced a desire for an organizational culture shift as well as specific means for centering community care, values alignment, and sustainability in daily work. Some voiced concern with the typical promotion of workplace-based self-care trends that put the onus on an individual to take better care of themselves in the face of stress and trauma-inducing realities of injustice. They felt practices should be integrated into the work so that changemakers do not feel like they must abandon their work in favor of their own healing and self-care. We might ask why we generally tend to burden the individual rather than work to change the societal norms and structures that perpetuate these stress- and trauma-inducing realities of injustice; even in well-intended organizations, the responsibility is most often put on individuals to adapt and become resilient to ineffective organizational policy and damaging societal influences.

It was brought up in our collective that one way toward both short-term and long-term change that could have tangible impacts was engaging in a cultural shift in organizations—really slowing down. In real-time, this impacts the number and scope of projects an organization takes on, the timelines attached to project deadlines, the expectations for output, and the pace for production. The benefits, according to existing research, are multifaceted. To slow down invites spaciousness not only for critical self-reflection, but also for resting, contemplating, stillness, healing, playing, awe, and connecting. This helps us feel better in our bodies, calms down our nervous systems, opens and deepens our connections with others, and allows our minds to generate new thoughts, make new connections between ideas, and develop new ways of conceiving the future. The activities of play, delight, pleasure, imagination, and creation are critical for our well-being, our capacity to innovate, and our ability to imagine the just and liberated world we are working toward. All of this feeds into whatever conversation, relationship, project, or work we do next, often with outcomes that are higher in quality and more innovative than when we were running on empty, trying to do more, faster.[13] To truly honor worker well-being, cultivate the capacity and space to imagine the world we want, and live in real-time values that defy toxic dominant norms, organizations must commit to a values-based shift in how they operate, evaluate, and organize time and related expectations.

However, intentionally choosing to slow down, do less, and rest requires us to go against capitalist conditioning around the use of time. There is a rest inequality along race and class lines, so slowing down also goes against inherently racist messages that bodies of color are meant for work and suffering, not relaxation and pleasure.[14] As Tricia Hersey, author of *Rest Is Resistance*, reminds us, "Rest pushes back and disrupts a system that views human bodies as a tool for production and labor. It is a counter-narrative."[15] As such, this example of a culture change is both an affirmation of a new direction organizations can take to be in better alignment with their values and an active resistance to dominant norms that produce stress and dis-ease disparately.

While changemakers repeatedly voiced the need to learn and implement new ways of doing business to address current challenges, our collective also overwhelmingly spoke to how new practices should leverage and expand the strengths that already exist in their communities. Since their communities are not wholly operating on a foundation of deficits, they desired to elevate the strength, resilience, and wisdom within changemaking organizations and engage existing community-care values and connections cultivated with both the staff within the organization and the communities they work with.

Changemakers voiced the need to talk candidly about both the need for and practical application of structural shifts in their organizations that would institutionalize the value of well-being in daily operations. One member reflected on the importance of talking to each other to bring about meaningful organizational change, noting: "I think courageous conversations are the first step always because we can bring in conversations about healing and meditation as much as we want, but as long as those [courageous conversations] haven't happened, I feel like it's gonna end up being superficial . . . and kind of like uplifting an image but not necessarily a reality."

Generally talking about the ideas of healing and self-care in social justice work or inviting a guest speaker or two on the topic is helpful, but the next and necessary step is to collectively reflect on what the organization needs and then prioritize regular practices and policies of well-being in the work. Members of our collective identified a number of possible practices to create culture shifts in organizations, including:

- Embedding trauma-informed, healing-centered frameworks and practices in the structure, policy, values, and culture of the organization, and utilizing professional development training, collective reflection, and accountability commitments to do so on individual and collective levels

- Prioritizing an intentional kind of work culture that gives time and value to

  - expressing candidly vulnerability around hardships in the work,
  - feedback for how support can be given and received,
  - setting boundaries clearly,
  - upholding accountability,
  - utilizing power intentionally in horizontal instead of hierarchical manners (i.e., power with/to/within rather than over), and
  - regularly engaging in rest, play, and repair[16]

- Facilitating routine listening circles, embodied well-being workshops, mindfulness exercises, and other community-building practices to build trust and feel connected within and across the community of workers

- Regularly reflecting on whether these policies and practices are making a difference to well-being and sustainability in the work

The need to have courageous conversations about practices within an organization that do not promote well-being, belonging, and equity is crucial to individual and organizational sustainability. Such conversations and structural changes need to be prioritized as the intention of time and commitment to such reflections can directly translate into changes in daily operations. One staff member in a leadership position spoke about her intentions to prioritize well-being for herself and her staff members in the organization but related that she was unsure if that was reflected in the actions of the organization: "I always try to say, 'Okay, what really matters first, right?' I always try to think in terms of [my coworkers'] well-being and my well-being first . . . but I don't know if that's actually relayed, and I think this is a good opportunity to explore that more."

A potential discrepancy exists between intended actions and what may occur in the moment. This member saw these conversations as an opportunity to understand if and how her intentions are being enacted and explored potential solutions of how to institutionalize values better in the organizational operations. Staff leadership values their coworkers' well-being, but without strong structural support for this, it can get lost in the urgency of the day-to-day work. Such change, at its core, requires a massive push-back on the reproduction of toxic norms of capitalism and neoliberalism that are replicated in the nonprofit industrial complex. This level of transformation of guiding principles and structures can certainly be overwhelming but also allows us to "rehearse the revolution" in real-time, community by community, organization by organization.[17]

Conclusion

The work of our Know Justice, Know Peace Collective revealed important themes regarding community care, healing, and organizational development, illuminating the dichotomy many changemakers experience in organizations fighting against—yet inevitably also reproducing—toxic norms that decrease or deny well-being and interconnection. Due to the urgency and heaviness of the traumas of injustice, many organizations often end up perpetuating hyperproductivity and debilitating stress while undervaluing trauma-informed healing and rest, resulting in a painful paradox and, often, decreased organizational impact and individual well-being. The desire to dismantle oppressive systems while also working for this change from within the limitations of nonprofit/capitalist culture creates sharp contradictions and exposes the necessity of connecting changes on individual levels to transformation on structural and systemic levels. Committing to greater investment in self, community, care, and integration of values for well-being and justice within organizational policy, culture, and structures continued to be the things that changemakers wanted more knowledge, skills, and practice around. The writers of this anthology aim to provide just that. If successful, together we can imagine a new world into being that can repair the harms of our collective past; regenerate traditions of healing and well-being that have been robbed, forgotten, or disposed of; and re-create new norms, structures, and systems in which we can live our justice and well-being values for personal and collective liberation.

2

THE TRAUMAS OF INJUSTICE

Understanding Trauma and Fostering Healing in Movement Work

Hala Khouri

We can bring down the entire system and have a worldwide revolution,
but if we haven't healed our traumas and learned how to be in authentic
relationships with each other, we will corrupt any new system we put in
its place.

—KAZU HAGA, *Healing Resistance*

Why Do We Need to Be Trauma Informed?

The most deleterious impact of the trauma of injustice is the loss of the ability to imagine and enact justice. As Kazu Haga said, even if we succeed in dismantling systems of oppression, we will inevitably re-create them if we have not attended to and healed our collective trauma.[1] Grounding ourselves in a trauma-informed framework can support a culture of healing in our organizations and collaborations. Justice cannot happen without healing, and trauma as well as toxic stress can get in the way of this process.

A trauma-informed framework is not meant to pathologize trauma-impacted communities and individuals; rather, it can shed light on the ways that unaddressed trauma can get in the way of healing and can even contribute to the retraumatization of people within our own movements. A paradigm of healing justice invites us to envision how our organizations might become a reflection of what we hope to see in the world. It's an invitation for us to practice justice and liberation together in an embodied and relational way.

At the heart of a trauma-informed approach is the call to center healing—personally, interpersonally, and collectively. Inside our movements for justice, the impact of systemic oppression and injustice can keep us in survival mode—constantly putting out fires and fighting for basic rights. This can make it feel impossible to have space to imagine what we want because all our energy is focused on dealing with the impacts of what we don't want. This is one aspect of the trauma of injustice—it can block our capacity to dream and imagine. When we center healing in our work toward justice, it can challenge and disrupt the ways we've become so accustomed to fighting that we get stuck and even unconsciously attached to the fight. When we center healing, our work can become generative rather than just reactive. This allows us to respond to harm as well as envision and work toward the radical transformation of our systems. This requires us to be flexible and agile as we move from crisis and urgent matters into spaces where we can connect and envision long-term solutions to the problems we are facing. In order to heal from the traumas of injustice, we must understand the impact of trauma on our communities and movements so we can create a new narrative together. Unspoken and unaddressed trauma often gets normalized as part of a person's personality or, for collective trauma, it can get coded as culture.[2] The healing process can help us transform the qualities and tendencies rooted in trauma and survival into more authentic and life-affirming traits that support us to move beyond survival and thrive.

Healing

The word *healing* can be ambiguous. What do we mean by healing? What are signs that we are healing? How do we create opportunities for healing while doing the often stressful and difficult work of fighting injustice or supporting people impacted by it? Understanding trauma and the impact of chronic and toxic stress can help us demystify the healing process so that we don't inadvertently get in our own way. In our work toward justice, healing can't just be about making the changes out in the world that are necessary; it must also be about being able to embody and enact justice with each other, inside our organizations, as we work toward that goal everywhere else. It is about cultivating affirming relationships and creating the conditions in which everyone can survive and thrive inside the microcosm of our organizations, collaborations, and relationships. Healing is also about transforming our trauma and pain into opportunities for meaningful growth. It is about fostering resilient communities and organizations that can handle the messiness of justice work, get good at apology and repair, and find ways to celebrate along the way.

Ultimately, healing is relational, but it also requires that we each do our personal work. This includes reflecting on what life experiences have shaped us and how they impact how we are in the world and with each other. You may have heard the expressions "You've got to name it to tame it" and "You have to feel it to heal it." This is why we start with trauma, for in the trauma is the opportunity for healing. Inside the wound is the potential for growth. When individuals are engaged in a process of authentic reflection to build self-awareness and accountability, they contribute toward the healing of their community. This radical self-awareness is a vital component of disrupting injustice; without it, we are likely to replicate the harmful dynamics of dominant culture that cause violence, division, and inequality.

Individual healing is not enough because, fundamentally, healing is also relational—it is about safety and belonging. It can be easy to fool ourselves into thinking that we are healed if we isolate ourselves from the world. Yet, we are social beings, and we need healthy, safe relationships in order to truly be well. As activists, many of us can use our activism to avoid our own vulnerability around relationships. We focus on fixing the world "out there" so we don't have to confront ourselves or make ourselves vulnerable. If our activism is a form of avoiding ourselves, we can't really be effective. Susan Raffo describes held trauma as "a moment of unfinished history. Life wants to come back to the present moment, to feel connected to other life. This means held trauma will find a way to resurface again and again until it is finished."[3] A healing justice paradigm asks us to be in alignment with our values on all levels—personally, interpersonally, and collectively.

In this chapter, I share a foundational framework for understanding how trauma impacts us and a pathway toward building a healing-centered culture that supports us to transform familiar cycles of trauma so we can embody and practice justice together in our organizations and alliances even before the broader culture has figured out how to do it.

Unpacking Trauma

Just because you've experienced trauma does not mean you're broken. Trauma shapes us, sometimes in beautiful ways and sometimes in awful ways, often both. Certain experiences or circumstances can buffer us against the negative impacts of trauma and stress, and others can leave us more vulnerable and at risk. One way to think about the things that buffer is as *resources*. Resources can be personal, interpersonal, material, spiritual, and systemic. I'm going to use my story as an example of how different kinds of resources can buffer an individual from being traumatized, even if they are experiencing a traumatic event.

I was born in Beirut, Lebanon, in 1973. I was two years old when war broke out, and although I don't remember much from that time, I am told stories of having to hide in our basement to avoid bombs. My father, who was a physician, would get picked up by an army tank to be taken to the hospital on the hill to see patients, and we would watch the tank go up the hill praying that nothing would go wrong along the way. Whenever we'd hear gunfire in the distance, my mom would tell my sister and me that it was fireworks for someone's birthday. Apparently, I'd tell her "I hope it isn't someone's birthday today" when I would get up in the morning. We were able to move to the US a year later when my father found a position at a hospital in Miami, Florida.

Being exposed to war at a young age is traumatic, yet I was not traumatized by that experience. Of course, it impacted me—in fact, I think it's the root of my motivation for much of my work today. However, I don't have significant trauma symptoms from the experience because I had many resources that served as protective factors. First, I had my family and a home that protected me and kept us all safe (interpersonal and material resources), and second, we had the means to leave after one year to build a life abroad (financial and educational resources, which are also connected to being advantaged on a systemic level due to our religious and class status). Those things buffered me from the potentially devastating effects of living in a war zone. As a result of that experience, I've been motivated to learn about trauma and justice, and I've dedicated my life to this work. I have a particular empathy and concern for trauma-impacted people and communities, and being an immigrant, I have my own experience of feeling othered and marginalized. I've also experienced light skin privilege, in addition to able-bodied, class, and education privilege.

Shock Trauma

At their core, traumatic events or circumstances overwhelm our capacity to cope and respond and leave us feeling helpless, hopeless, and out of control. *Shock traumas* are things that happen *to* us—like violence, rape, war, car accidents, natural disasters, witnessing violence, and even medical procedures. These can be singular events or chronic and repeated. They are terrorizing ruptures in our reality that challenge the foundation beneath us and can disrupt our ability to function. (They can also expand our capacity and transform us in positive ways.) Trauma is not the event; it is the response to the event. It is what stays with us long after the event is over. This has to do with our physiological response to threats and how our nervous system can hold onto, or let go of, the survival energy mobilized to deal with a traumatic event.

When human animals encounter a threat, such as a bear about to attack us, we instinctively mobilize to deal with it. We go into sympathetic arousal or a fight-or-flight state. In this state, our body secretes excitatory chemicals and hormones, our heart rate goes up, breathing gets shallow, digestion shuts down, and energy rushes to our extremities so we can fight off the threat or run away. If we successfully run away or fight, we utilize the energy that was mobilized and thus release it from our nervous system. In an ideal situation, we deal with the threat and are able to return to a resting state. We are able to move on and leave the event behind us. This event, as scary as it seemed, does not traumatize us because we were able to cope and respond.

But what if we can't cope? What if we can't run or fight? Another response to a threat is the freeze response. Freeze is like having the accelerator and the brakes pushed at the same time. We're flooded with stress energy yet immobilized in the moment. Freeze is an adaptive response because, sometimes, if the predator doesn't see us or thinks we're dead, it leaves us untouched. Appeasement can also fall into this category; this is when we comply to minimize a potential threat. In this case, whether we freeze, appease, or try to escape or fight but are unsuccessful, we do not have the experience of being able to cope and respond. We are not able to utilize the energy that was mobilized to deal with the threat, and that energy stays stuck inside of us. The chemicals that get secreted when we experience a threat are meant to be a short-term strategy to keep us alive; when trauma is not resolved, it has a deleterious impact on our capacity to feel settled and safe. This can lead to trauma symptoms such as anxiety, hypervigilance, depression, or shutdown. It can look like insomnia, flashbacks, or always feeling like there's a bear around the corner waiting for you. The survival response that was meant to be temporary can become constant. As the title of the best-selling book on trauma by Bessel van der

Kolk, *The Body Keeps the Score,* indicates, we carry the imprints of our life experiences in our bodies, and they can keep us stuck in the past until we heal.

Peter Levine, creator of Somatic Experiencing, found that animals in the wild have a way of discharging the energy that was mobilized to deal with a traumatic event that prevents them from being traumatized by predator attacks.[4] Animals will shake and tremble after an encounter with a predator and release the energy and impulses that they weren't able to act on. Most humans have been socialized out of this response. We've been told by the dominant culture to get over it and move on, suck it up, don't complain, and get back to being productive (some call this the trauma of capitalism).[5] We've been told not to cry, scream, shake, or act "wild." In many ways, we have civilized ourselves away from our innate capacity to heal from trauma.

Most of our Indigenous ancestors had healing rituals that included dancing, shaking, sounding, and other practices to release and express their trauma, grief, rage, and even joy. One of the mechanisms of colonization and white supremacy was to cut people off from their Indigenous healing practices. People were killed if they were found doing these practices, and while plenty of these practices were suppressed, many have continued despite the efforts to exterminate them. For numerous reasons, many of us don't follow our body's natural instinct to release trauma. Instead, we suppress and hold onto it, which has an impact on our well-being and on our capacity to work toward justice sustainably. Embodied practices to release stress and trauma are a vital part of healing, and we can bring them into our organizations to support our work for justice.[6]

Developmental Trauma

Another category of trauma is not caused by a discrete event or events; rather, it is relational. *Developmental trauma* is caused by an ongoing misattunement between a child and their primary caregiver. Human

43

babies rely on their caregivers to survive. If the caregiver is not attuned and responsive to the child's needs, both physically and emotionally, the child will feel overwhelmed and thus helpless and hopeless in the world. Emotional abuse, neglect, and severe inconsistency in behavior can all be traumatic to infants and young children. We are relational beings, and our attachments with our caregivers leave a lifelong imprint on us that affects all our future relationships, for better or for worse. When we are ignored or unseen as children, it has a dramatic impact on our capacity to feel safe, connected, and embodied. When we are not able to develop secure attachments with our caregivers, it can be hard to develop healthy, secure attachments as adults.

People with developmental trauma tend to be more anxious or avoidant in their relationships. Some people have very poor boundaries and are more vulnerable to abuse and manipulation; others have overly strong boundaries and isolate or become abusive themselves. Ultimately, developmental trauma can make it difficult to have healthy, balanced relationships and can impede our sense of connection and belonging. "Trauma compromises our ability to engage with others by replacing patterns of connection with patterns of protection," says Stephen Porges, trauma researcher and creator of Polyvagal Theory.[7] Porges's research has validated what many already know—one of the biggest ways that unhealed trauma impacts us is in our capacity to feel safe with others. We all need to feel safe, included, and valued. For people with a history of developmental trauma, this can feel impossible. We heal developmental trauma inside of relationships where all parties are committed to disrupting unhealthy habits and nurturing healthy ones.

The Trauma of Injustice: Systemic Trauma

A final major category of trauma is systemic trauma, which refers to violence, inequality, and oppression that is perpetuated, sanctioned, and upheld on structural and institutional levels. These systems include education, healthcare, the criminal legal system, politics, finance, and public policy. These systems favor certain individuals and communities and exclude, disregard, or even harm others, often based on their identity. This results in what can be seen as the *trauma of injustice* and includes racism, ableism, sexism, cissexism, heterosexism, classism, xenophobia, religious bigotry, and any other form of identity-based injustice. Many different forms of shock and developmental trauma can be a result of injustice directly or indirectly.

When these forms of discrimination are internalized by individuals, they can be upheld by the culture without needing external reinforcement by the broader systems. This can look like someone from a targeted group not feeling like they deserve the same treatment and rights that someone from a dominant group is afforded (this is called *internalized oppression*). Those individuals may not push back when treated unfairly both because of what they have internalized and because of the potential consequences of pushing back (freeze/appease response). At the same time, people whose identities are privileged by the dominant culture can take it to be normal or their birthright to receive certain benefits (*internalized dominance*) and they may not even think to push back or challenge this assumption.

The traumas of injustice include shock trauma such as identity-based violence, deportation, incarceration, and life-altering experiences of discrimination or bias. Injustice and oppression can also be a cause of developmental trauma such as when a parent/caregiver cannot be there to attune to a child due to incarceration or deportation, unresolved traumas of their own, or when a person's identity is pathologized, marginalized, or made invisible by the broader culture and systems (such as someone who is neurodivergent, gender nonconforming, or has a visible or invisible disability).

Social justice is often framed in terms of access to resources and proximity to power. While a lack of resources and power can certainly be traumatic, it can also fall into a category of chronic and toxic stress. Living under sustained periods of high stress can impact people just as trauma does. This can range from the stress of living in a poor neighborhood—which often exposes people to air and water pollution, noise pollution, and consistent fears of violence—the stress of dealing with a healthcare system that may not care for you or your loved ones, or the stress of having an education system that doesn't meet your needs. Even stressors around transportation, childcare, and access to fresh food can be intense enough to have a serious impact.

Contrast this with the experience of being served by the systems around you. Privilege is often invisible to those experiencing it—they are accustomed to having their needs met without having to struggle or fight. This privilege becomes a "buffer zone," as Sara Ahmed says. She goes on to point out

> *When a whole world is organized to promote your survival, from health to education, from the walls designed to keep your residence safe, from the paths that ease your travel, you do not have to become so inventive to survive. You do not have to be seen as the recipient of welfare because the world has promoted your welfare. The benefits you receive are given as entitlements, perhaps even as birth rights.*[8]

Our identities are complex, and we may find we benefit in certain settings or in relationship to certain structures while we are targeted in others. The categories I'm offering here are not meant to be exhaustive or rigid. I offer them so that we can create some distinctions around the various sources of trauma and thus the various sources of healing. We also want to be cautious not to engage in an "oppression Olympics" where we compete to prove who has more trauma or privilege. This is not useful and pits us against each other unnecessarily. The truth is, someone can be at the top of the social hierarchy but still have experienced horrific trauma, and someone can be at the bottom of the social hierarchy and have been buffered from the negative effects of it. Many communities not served by the broader system are incredibly resilient; they have developed their own support systems that can strengthen family and community ties, create a strong sense of meaning and purpose, and ultimately foster a sense of wholeness and hope that are massively protective. Conversely, people with a lot of systemic and material privilege can feel isolated and disconnected from a sense of community and purpose because they can afford to hire people to support them instead of leaning on loved ones for support. They may also feel like they don't have the right to struggle so they hide behind a veneer of being "fine" when they really need support. Regardless of social location, when systemic trauma and toxic stress are not directly addressed, they can limit the impact we have in social change work and our own capacity for healing and joy.

Trauma-Informed and Healing-Centered Organizational Culture

At its core, the goal of a trauma-informed culture is to foster individual and community healing and resilience by centering our shared humanity. The word *resilience* can refer to our capacity to overcome adversity or to rebound from difficulty. It can point to people's strength and capacity as well as their ingenuity and determination. Humans are amazing; we can, and have, overcome the unimaginable. The term can also be misused and weaponized. For example, it can be used to imply that if someone does not triumph over trauma, they have fallen short. Often folks fail to ask why certain people have had to be so resilient to survive while others haven't. In his critical book *Hope and Healing in Urban Education*, Shawn Ginwright asks why we spend so much time talking about being more resilient rather than talking about how to change the systemic harm that requires such tremendous resilience of us in the first place.[9]

Collective Resilience

I agree with the concerns about the way *resilience* can be misused, and I want to reframe it as being beyond a personal attribute and as something we do together when we build cultures and organizations that can hold complexity and withstand difficulty. Resilience isn't perfection; it's about doing our best to make meaning of our suffering and growing our hearts because of it. It's also about building our capacity for accountability and repair. It's about being vulnerable, flexible, and strong, all at once. Doing work connected to justice requires a lot of resilience in the face of trauma.

Shawn Ginwright and Angel Acosta, among others, have also invited us to move away from the term *trauma-informed* and talk about being *healing-centered* instead.[10] This can help disrupt the ways marginalized communities are often identified with their deficits rather than their assets. I believe that understanding trauma can help us move beyond it skillfully so we can focus on an asset-based framework of healing.

There is no linear process toward building a healing-centered culture. The process of culture building is ongoing and never ends, especially when we're trying to create something that challenges dominant cultural norms. The broader culture constantly pulls us away from healing, so we must be persistent inside our organizations and collectives. As adrienne maree brown says, social change is *emergent*. In her book *Emergent Strategy*, she explains "emergent strategy, strategy for building complex patterns and systems of change through relatively small interactions, is to me, the potential scale of transformation that could come from movements intentionally practicing this adaptive, relational way of being, on our own and with others."[11]

Our job is to create the conditions for change to happen and to recognize that this starts with us as individuals and as collectives doing the work together. Because *how can we expect the rest of the world to be what we cannot be with each other?*

Understanding trauma is just the start. Being trauma-informed/healing-centered in our work can look different in different settings. Yet all of us must cultivate critical consciousness and embodied tools for reflection and accountability in order to create these conditions together.

Critical Consciousness

The term *critical* is rooted in critical theory, and its many iterations refer to the awareness of the role of power in shaping us. A critical culture aims to push against the misuse of power and to address power imbalances and corruption. This requires critical consciousness and a commitment to introspection on all levels of an organization. Paulo Freire coined the term *conscientization*, or critical consciousness, to refer to our awareness of the sociopolitical context that shapes us.[12] A healing justice paradigm asks us to consider what has impacted us on a personal, interpersonal, and systemic level and how that influences our actions, perceptions, and relationships. It also invites us to structure our organizations around norms and practices that allow us to work together in a way that doesn't replicate harmful dynamics so our work together can be authentic, effective, and transformative.

We are all carrying various combinations of experiences inside our bodies, minds, and hearts. Some of us have experienced developmental and systemic trauma, others may only know shock trauma in our lives, and some of us have never encountered major trauma directly. All of us have different levels of resources or things that buffer or protect us from the deleterious effects of traumatic situations. We are all shaped by these life experiences and circumstances, and this influences how we move through the world. Becoming aware of this and continuing to investigate the impact of our own lived experiences on our feelings, thoughts, and actions are key components for building a healing culture and having a greater impact in our work for justice.

The following is an example of what this can look like.

■ ■ ■

In 2020, I was asked to facilitate some work at a domestic violence agency. This agency had six locations and served thousands of people. Not only did they have shelters for families escaping violence, but they also offered a robust number of services such as therapy, childcare, job training and placement, and housing support. This agency was also dedicated to centering the voices of survivors in their programs and they had several programs that were survivor-led. Senior leaders asked me to come because they had noticed some very negative dynamics among the team members, and morale was low for everyone in the organization. The staff was resentful of the senior leaders; they felt like they were expected to work too many hours for the pay they received. They felt discarded and disrespected and like they had no voice in the organization even though they were the ones spending the most time with the participants. They perceived senior leaders as being selfish and not caring about them. Also, a lot of conflict among the staff was exacerbated by gossip and poor communication. Meanwhile, the executive director and the leadership team were irritated with the staff. They worked tirelessly to raise money for the organization, chasing grant opportunities, dealing with pressure from their board, and feeling the weight of the whole organization on their shoulders. They perceived the staff as being ungrateful, selfish, and unwilling to work hard.

This is a common dynamic that occurs in organizations structured in this way. Often the people at the top—the executive director and the senior leadership team—don't communicate directly with the staff on the ground (in this case the people who worked inside the shelters where the families stayed as well as the caseworkers and therapists). At the agency I visited, supervisors often felt caught in the middle; they had to answer to the senior team while working with the staff. Even the participants were acting out—they didn't trust the staff at the shelters, some weren't showing up for therapy, and others reported feeling unsupported. The negativity was impacting everyone.

Money and time always feel scarce in organizations like this, and the culture is typically one of urgency, stress, and chaos. This is the case for many real reasons, especially in this organization, which served mostly undocumented people who were dealing with violence in the home and for whom the threat of deportation was always looming. The people inside this organization all had huge hearts, and they came to this work because they cared for the people they served; it was heartbreaking to see how many people ended up shut down, resentful, and disconnected because of the pressure and stressful work environment (which can make the larger issues they are fighting feel insurmountable). In many organizations facing similar circumstances, people can project overwhelming feelings onto the people they work with, and they blame those who are on their side for their disappointment and pain. This is what I saw when I spoke to various team members at the domestic violence agency. Everyone I spoke to cared deeply about the community they were serving. Many of them had their own experience with intimate partner violence, which made them even more invested. Yet internal conflict and stress were creating an environment of mistrust and doubt between people who all shared the same vision—to eradicate domestic violence.

In one of my sessions with the entire team, we did an exercise from a body of work called *Theatre of the Oppressed*, developed by Augusto Boal. His work is designed to reveal and then help shift conditions of oppression toward conditions for liberation. In this exercise, one person stands at the front of what ends up being a triangle of people. Two people stand behind them, then four behind them, and so on. Each person puts their hands on the shoulders of two people in front of them so everyone is connected. The person at the very front is instructed to walk around the space; meanwhile, everyone behind them must keep contact with the two people in front of them. At one point, I stand about twenty feet in front of the group and yell to the person in the front, "If you can get here in five seconds, you'll get a $50,000 grant!" This causes the person to run toward me, which often results in the people in the back being whipped around and losing connection with the people in front of them. Sometimes the group has to take twists and turns to hit the mark I've set for them, which is even more disruptive to the group. Every few minutes, I have people find a new location within the shape.

At the end, when we debriefed, people shared that when they were in the back, they didn't know what was going on; they were upset at the people in the front for making them have to run so fast, without any warning, so that they almost tripped or lost connection with the others. People shared that when they were in the front, they felt responsible for everyone behind them but were only focused on the urgent goals ahead of them. They didn't think to turn and communicate with those behind them because there wasn't any time. The people in the middle said they could see what was happening in the front but didn't have any time to warn those in the back.

As you can see, this exercise represents the dynamics that can occur in top-down structures. What was particularly fascinating to me was that when I would put a staff member at the front, they acted just like the senior leaders. They rushed toward goals, didn't communicate with the folks in the back, and were frustrated when people couldn't keep up. And when senior leaders were at the back, they felt mistreated and resentful of those in the front for not extending the care and concern they felt they deserved. What the group saw from this exercise is that many of the negative dynamics in the organization are not due to individual people's intentions, but to the structures in place both inside the organization and in the broader world that don't support places like this to be sustainable, well funded, and cared for. They were able to see that when they were put in a different position, they also responded in a way that they criticized others for. This is one important part of critical consciousness—to reflect on how the systems that we are a part of influence us. This can help us see when the problem is the structure, not the individual.

To add to this complexity, we also know that individuals bring their own personal history and social identity to the roles they occupy. All too often in nonprofit organizations people in senior positions come from a different class and racial background than the communities they are working in. This requires an added responsibility on their part to reflect on what they might bring to their position. In this particular organization, the executive director was a Latina woman who had been a participant at the organization when she was experiencing domestic violence. Even still, her staff projected onto her and she became frustrated by that. This is how powerful structural dynamics are.

As a result of this work, the members of this team, at all levels of the organization, were able to step back and have some empathy for their colleagues. They were also able to see that many of their feelings about each other were not personal at all. The group began communicating more across all levels of leadership. Senior leadership realized that they had a particular responsibility to set a tone of respect and empathy for the whole team, even if they were stressed and overwhelmed; they had to prioritize opportunities for everyone in the organization to feel heard and seen. They had to be clear and honest about when people had decision-making power and when they didn't. They also had to prioritize the well-being of their team, even if that meant losing some grants or missing out on other opportunities. They created an advisory team with representatives from all levels of the organization that would meet quarterly to share their feedback and recommendations. Everyone in the organization received training on active listening and nonviolent communication as well as on somatic practices for self-regulation and self-care. People were encouraged to understand that although their feelings were real, they were not always accurate, and these practices could give them some tools to skillfully navigate their working relationships.

It's important to note that before offering the staff tools for self-care and self-regulation, senior leadership had to take responsibility for their lack of communication and how they dealt with the chaos and urgency. If leadership didn't address this, the staff could feel like they were being asked to breathe their way through an unfair and untenable situation. Building a culture that values everyone's well-being takes a lot of work; it requires ongoing culture building to normalize the practices that push against the traumatic patterns of dominant culture and amplify our capacity to be connected and resilient in the face of stress and trauma.

Dynamics like this are present in every organization. The question is not *if* dominant culture and our conditioning are impacting our organizations, but *how* they are and what we can do about it. A healing-centered paradigm invites us to make visible and challenge the invisible dynamics that are impacting our perceptions and behaviors. When we can identify them, we can address them with more skill and effectiveness. This is messy! When it's not, it's likely we are oversimplifying the issues to avoid conflict. Binary thinking can have us constantly pointing fingers to see who is to blame—who is more oppressed, who is more traumatized, who is more harmed, who has more power, who is seen as the other. This can show up in spaces dedicated to disrupting injustice in an attempt to make visible the impact of oppression and injustice. Yet, if left unchecked, we simply flip the script and create a new hierarchical culture that is divisive and competitive and perpetuates trauma and domination. What is probably our most revolutionary act today is working for justice by working for internal and external healing, connection, and resilience.

Embodiment

Our bodies hold our stories. They carry the power and grace we acquire through our life experiences as well as the energy of trauma that is unresolved, unexpressed, and unmetabolized. Our body is our guidance system. It's like a GPS device—when it's properly calibrated, it gives us accurate information about the outside world and how to move through it; it can guide us to where we want to be and how we want to be. One of the main roles of our autonomic nervous system is to alert us to when there's danger and we should retreat or fight and when we're safe and we can settle. When we are overburdened with trauma or stress, our body's signals can be unreliable and erratic. We get stuck in survival mode and defense. One word for this is *dysregulation*. This means that we are stuck in activation or shutdown, or we go back and forth from one extreme to the other. It's like having alarm bells constantly ringing inside of us, or, the opposite, we are shut down, numb, and feeling nothing. When we are in our survival brain, our thinking (and feeling) is black and white. This can lead to conflict and poor communication. It's almost impossible to have nuance and see multiple sides to a situation when we're dysregulated, and it becomes very hard to relate to others and communicate effectively when we are constantly in this state. When we can settle ourselves, we can collaborate, be accountable, communicate skillfully, get creative, and be more effective in our work together.

In addition to connecting us to what is going on inside of us, somatic practices can help us manage the overwhelm that can come when we reconnect to our emotions. When we can feel settled in the face of intense emotions (both ours and those of other people), we are more likely to navigate the situation in a way that is better for everyone involved. Simple things like encouraging people to breathe, stretch, and check in with themselves can change the energy of a meeting or a one-on-one interaction. Understanding when we are triggered can allow us to take a moment to settle before we engage with someone; when we are settled, our communication will be more skillful. When everyone inside an organization understands that we are all carrying something and that when we frontload curiosity and empathy for each other, we can find ways of being in the stress and chaos that don't have us turning on each other.

Embodied practices build up our capacity to be with discomfort without going into a trauma response. Trauma responses cause us to blame, shame, project, shut down, or lash out. They are never useful (unless you're in an actual traumatic situation). This is especially important when doing work around social justice because this work exposes us to traumatic situations and circumstances. These practices allow us to stay connected to each other amid the chaos so we can be part of the solution.

Several years ago, I was asked to train the entire staff at a youth residential treatment center so they could offer trauma-informed/ equity-centered care to their residents. The people in the room were clinicians, educators, administrators, and all support staff. One exercise we did was a simple hip stretch sitting in our chairs. I invited people to go to the first edge of sensation and notice any feelings or thoughts that came up. I explained to them that our bodies can hold onto painful emotions, and allowing ourselves to connect with our sensations can help us feel what we might be holding onto so we can release it. During the debrief, Ramon, a security guard who often was tasked with chasing a kid who was trying to run away, shared that he started crying during that stretch, and this took him by surprise. Ramon confessed that he often felt angry and frustrated at the youth who tried to run away. He struggled with substance use as a teen but never got the care and support these young people had access to. So, when they acted out, he perceived them to be ungrateful.

Ramon didn't realize how much sadness and grief he was holding onto. Sadness for himself as a youth and the lack of support around him, and sadness for these young people struggling in the same way he did. When I spoke to Ramon a few weeks later, he shared that his attitude toward the youth had shifted and that he was feeling much less stressed and on edge in general. He attributed this to starting each day with some simple stretches and breathing exercises, and he was slowly getting in the habit of tracking his own sensations and emotions throughout the day. He noticed that he was feeling a lot more empathy for the residents. Even though he still could get frustrated with them, he now knew what was beneath the frustration and it allowed him to be more patient and kinder.

Somatic practices can help us develop an embodied intelligence and capacity in a few ways. First, they foster interoception. *Interoception* refers to our ability to sense what is happening inside of us. Just like Ramon, many of us move through our lives disconnected from our own sensations; this may be because of trauma, overwhelm, or just a culture that encourages distraction and disembodiment. Reconnecting to our emotions, impulses, and sensations allows us to be aware of what is going on for us. Only from this place of radical self-awareness can we take accountability for our actions and motivations. Without self-awareness, we're more likely to blame others and lash out or shame ourselves and lash in.

Somatic practices can also help us get resources and stay grounded in the face of intense emotion and stress. This can allow us to be responsive rather than reactive as well as flexible and adaptive in the face of stress so that we can pivot when needed, stay open to new ideas, and be willing to be uncomfortable, which is required for growth to occur.

Conclusion

When we practice self-awareness (critical consciousness) and use embodied strategies to regulate our nervous system and engage with each other, this lays the foundation for effective communication, collaboration, and healthy relationships. Being healing-centered means prioritizing relationships inside of our organizations as well as with the communities and individuals we are working with. Of course, organizations need to create policies and systems that allow the people working inside of them to cultivate these practices. This includes looking at HR policies to make sure they are fair and conducive to a work/life balance. It also means examining hiring practices, who has decision-making power, and even the way space is set up to be truly accessible.[13] This requires ongoing and explicit work that affirms the values of a trauma-informed/healing-centered paradigm. This means everyone in an organization (from the board to the front-desk staff) needs to be engaged in this work. With power comes different responsibilities, and having a nuanced and discerning plan in place that takes that into consideration is vital.

There's no one way to build a trauma-informed culture. This is ongoing work that must evolve and adapt as an organization and its members change and grow. Organizations and collaboratives that genuinely embrace this approach will find a decrease in burnout and conflict and an increase in hopefulness and capacity. It's difficult work that can be very confronting, but it's necessary for both the longevity and success of our efforts toward healing and justice in our communities and the world at large.

3

MICRO TO MACRO

Embodied Trauma-Informed and Resilience-Oriented Systems Change

Nkem Ndefo

We have to imagine the kind of society we want to inhabit. We can't simply assume that somehow, magically, we're going to create a new society in which there will be new human beings. No, we have to begin that process of creating the society we want to inhabit right now.

—ANGELA Y. DAVIS

To capture the wide breadth and fine detail of my systems change work, it is not enough for me to present didactic theory and describe the large clashing forces of oppression and liberation. It is equally important to share the practical and the personal. I start this chapter with an illustrative case study (italicized) and then turn to explanatory text. I return to the same case over and over, folding in the big ideas and practical guidance at relevant junctures. As you read, I invite you to slow down and notice what questions arise and how your emotions and body respond to each part of the case study. And when you arrive at the theoretical sections, I invite you to notice if your questions get answered and your emotional and somatic responses make more sense.

■ ■ ■

A big part of my work in the world is with an organization I founded to shepherd individuals, communities, and organizations through healing and liberatory change processes. Recently, my team and I were asked to design an educational program to improve cultural responsiveness and to create more humane permit and city code enforcement in a new street vending program. After vendors began to publicly share abusive enforcement experiences, a collective of activist and advocate organizations got enough attention from city leadership to mandate that Bureau of Street Services field investigators be trained along with a legislative initiative to make the vending permitting process more equitable. When my team was brought onto the training part of the project, I knew that in order to design a relevant curriculum, I needed to understand the perspectives and experiences of both the street vendors and the investigators. I learned about the vendors from the advocate collective, but I needed more information about the law enforcement side. So, I asked to ride along with the investigators as they interacted with the vendors.

On the day of the ride-along, I was paired with a vendor advocate who was tasked with providing me with more contextual explanations and any language interpretation I needed. Together we stood back and observed how the investigators provided vendors with education about legal requirements and wrote the occasional warning or citation. I took every opportunity to talk with the investigators about their job frustrations, hopes, and needs—to really understand their motivations for doing the work. Building an empathy bridge is vital to creating an educational process capable of not just providing knowledge but shifting attitudes and behavior.

A few times, the advocate would hang back and talk with the vendors to make sure they understood their rights. The situation took a turn when the advocate started peppering the investigators with questions about the real difficulties vendors faced getting permits. The investigators repeatedly stated that they had no control of the street vending permit process and were simply tasked with educating vendors about the rules and enforcing existing laws. The advocate became increasingly agitated. One of the investigators became teary under aggressive and accusatory questioning as he insisted that he had no power to change the system and was trying to educate people so they could vend legally and safely. I intervened to apologize to the investigators and to re-explain the purpose of the ride-along. I then pulled the advocate aside into a private conversation.

The advocate had plenty of reasons to be frustrated and angry based on the history of abusive investigator behavior, but none of that was happening that day with these particular investigators. His inability to contain his very legitimate emotions led him to sabotage the goal of the entire ride-along. Trust was ruptured instead of us building the connection necessary for an educational program that could effectively foster investigator empathy for the vendors—empathy necessary for investigators to implement culturally responsive and humane permit enforcement while advocates were concurrently working with the legislature to transform the governing laws.

What went wrong here? How did advocacy sabotage the program's strategic goals? A problem of poor timing and focus, yes. But the more important questions are "Why did an advocate who wanted humane, culturally responsive treatment for street vendors explode on the investigators he needed to convert into allies?" and "What might be needed for the advocate to stay simultaneously connected to his own valid emotional experience, the humanity of the investigators, and the strategy to create equitable systems change?"

■ ■ ■

The activist collective brought me and my team into this project because we had a local track record of successfully infusing a social justice perspective into organizational and systems change work. From projects with small community-based organizations to large-scale healthcare systems, we use what we have come to call an *embodied trauma-informed resilience-oriented (eTIRO) approach*. Although its parent model trauma-informed care was originally developed to improve mental healthcare, we recognized that it had the bones to be a liberatory framework for change.

First codified by the Substance Abuse and Mental Health Services Administration (SAMHSA), a United States federal government agency, trauma-informed care expanded the defining scope of trauma from a purely physical or psychological experience to one that encompassed the historical and current reality inherent in enduring systems of oppression. SAMHSA recognized that modifying mental health treatment models for individual patients was not sufficient without completely transforming the structure and culture of behavioral healthcare organizations for patients and staff alike. SAMHSA offered trauma-informed care as a model to achieve a four-fold goal: 1) to realize the widespread impact of trauma and understand potential paths for recovery; 2) to recognize the manifestations of trauma in clients, families, staff, and others involved with the system; 3) to fully integrate knowledge about trauma into policies, procedures, and practices; and 4) to actively resist retraumatization.[1] To successfully realize these goals, SAMHSA delineated six key principle clusters: safety; trustworthiness and transparency; peer support; collaboration and mutuality; empowerment, voice, and choice; and cultural, historical, and gender issues. Taken together, these goals and principles foster a compassionate organizational culture of equity, inclusion, and justice.

It would be remiss of me to overlook the roots of trauma-informed care, which can be traced through several confluent and mutually interacting traditions and movements: the collective and community orientation of Indigenous, non-Western, and faith-based traditions; the advocacy around shared experience and deep stakeholder involvement from the community health worker and peer mental health movements; the reclamation of sovereign community-rooted approaches of mutual aid groups; and the understanding of the intersection between individual trauma and systems of oppression centered by anti-gender-based-violence advocates. Additionally, in the fifteen years prior to SAMHSA's publication of their seminal guide to trauma-informed care, groundbreaking neuroscience and public health research documented the somatic nature of the trauma experience and the interconnections between traumatic exposure and impaired neurodevelopment with resulting wide-ranging chronic physical and psychological harms.

As interest in trauma-informed care grew in the behavioral health sector, funding and policy mandates increased programming for trauma-informed patient care but failed to recognize that trauma is often "a unifying aspect in the lives of those who run the organization, who provide the services, and/or who come to the organization for assistance and support."[2] Not only was the lived experience of trauma in leadership and staff routinely ignored, but trauma-informed initiatives usually failed to heed SAMHSA's call for comprehensive trauma-informed organizational development. As the trauma-informed approach spread to physical healthcare, social services, education, and even legal/carceral settings, this same focus on the end user (patient, client, student, incarcerated person, respectively) to the exclusion of the organizational structure and the people providing care and services continued. Ironically, even staff wellness initiatives designed to increase productivity and mitigate burnout largely overlooked how holistic trauma-informed organizational development could improve the well-being of the entire organizational ecosystem.

When we saw how open organizations were to trauma-informed programming for their end users and their simultaneous desire to support staff wellness, my team saw an opportunity to braid these two threads together by returning to SAMHSA's original intent for organizational culture and systems change. However, we found that although teaching about the impact and manifestations of trauma is a core component of trauma-informed care, using a purely cognitive didactic model ignores the actual reality of how to support traumatized people's learning, let alone their capacities to effect systems change.

■ ■ ■

When I pulled the street vendor advocate aside into that private conversation, he poured out his frustration and bitterness after years of witnessing the struggles immigrant street vendors endured at the hands of indifferent bureaucrats, NIMBY residents,[3] hostile business owners, and abusive law

enforcement. When I asked him about his dreams for change, he spoke pas-
sionately of a reformed permitting and enforcement system that treated the
vendors with dignity, but he quickly slipped back into seething anger. Again,
his anger was a righteous one, yet it overwhelmed him.

■ ■ ■

We need a certain fight energy to dismantle the interlocking systems of oppression—settler colonialism, white supremacy, capitalism, hetero-patriarchy, ableism, and ageism. Activists and change agents use this energy to identify and challenge the ways that oppressions manifest in our governments, schools, organizations, and healthcare systems through codified hierarchies, statutes, and policies that mutually reinforce infor-mal procedures and processes, relational dynamics, and cultural norms. Interrogation, critique, and subversion of dominant narratives, structures, and ways of being require judgment and a focus on what is wrong. They require uprooting, tearing down, blowing up, smashing, protesting, defy-ing, fighting. The spirit is urgent, confrontational, and destructive. And it is necessary to interrupt harm.

When we apply an embodied lens to dismantling energy, it allows us to bring in learnings from the neurophysiology and psychology of human defense responses. For instance, we know that threat activates a cascade of internal changes marked by a flood of adrenaline. This leads us to feel a global experience of pressure, reactivity, and need to mobilize rather than feeling present and connected. However useful this fight energy is for protection and subversion of oppressive systems, it comes with its own dangers when employed in situations that either don't warrant a fight reaction or ask for a more nuanced response. Defense responses are built to hijack our whole beings in service of preserving life, livelihood, and self. Biologic urgency can collapse strategic thinking and create rigid binaries that impair access to flexible problem-solving. The survival instinct narrows concern to self-preservation at the expense of the larger collective, and in the extreme, it dehumanizes those different from us. It numbs both our internal experience and shared humanity, which allows the control and domination inherent in the systems of oppression themselves to replicate.

This fight energy is very different from the spirit we need to reimagine liberatory worlds where we thrive. It is more than imagining but rather, as my coconspirators at Healing Justice London say, *rehearsing freedoms*— being and relating to one another in ways that sustainably create equity, support interdependence, celebrate difference, nurture creativity, savor pleasure, and provide nourishing rest. Dreaming and building are spacious and generative processes in which we need to be able to hold multiple complexities and remain settled enough in our bodies to connect to our interiority without letting our perspectives and needs eclipse those of others. The biology of a settled nervous system supports the psychology and behaviors that afford easy social connection and communication. We physiologically hear one another better as our ears tune to the range of the human voice. The gentle slowing of the parasympathetic nervous system creates space, time, and flexibility in thinking and actions. Rest becomes restorative, supporting energetic sustainability.

Systems change requires the spirit of both dismantling and building, but we need the self-knowledge to determine whether we are in the dismantling or building energy, the wisdom to discern when to engage which energy, and the skills to shift our states fluidly. These are embodied capacities. Because we are in the land of the psychological, behavioral, *and* physiological, purely cognitive-based approaches will not suffice. Recognizing and quieting the tell-tale signs of adrenaline-fueled thinking and reactions in real-time is critical to being able to pull out of a needlessly aggressive exchange with a colleague. Defense responses don't respond to controlling mental logic; rather, they need mind-body strategies like mindfulness, movement, and breath. Again, these are embodied capacities.

It's important to note that survival energy exacts a heavy metabolic and psychic toll, especially when overactivated for prolonged periods of time. Systems change work is long-haul work. So, when we identify when a response is maladaptive and settle unnecessary reactions, we conserve energy for greater sustainability so we can go the distance. And within the work, when we attune our responses to the needs of the moment, we are better able to be strategic and effective in both dismantling and building activities. We have an embodied resilience to navigate adversity and the bandwidth to change systems of inequity and oppression into places where we thrive. This is what I call *alchemical resilience* and it is missing from existing conceptions of trauma-informed care.

While trauma-informed care provides a framework for holistic systems change, when we fail to account for the need for alchemical resilience, we end up asking more of people without giving them the internal knowledge and skills they need to effect change. It is inhumane to expect leaders and the workforce to create a safe trauma-informed environment for colleagues and the systems' end users when everyone is living in the same interlocking network of oppressions and often sharing similar traumas. The first trauma-informed principle is safety, and it is not something that we can create in our mind; it is a felt experience of the body. If leaders and the workforce do not know how to access internal safety, they will infuse fear into policies and procedures that will reflect compliance in lieu of collaboration.

Having witnessed this poor implementation of trauma-informed care, I worked with my team to create a dynamic model for individual and collective transformation, an embodied trauma-informed resilience-oriented (eTIRO) approach. When we integrate embodiment and foundational focus in building alchemical resilience into trauma-informed care, we allow eTIRO to address organizational transformation from the innermost domains—intrapersonal and interpersonal—to the collective and systemic dimensions. While eTIRO has many of the same bones of traditional trauma-informed care, the work starts when we intentionally frontload leadership and staff capacity building using the Resilience Toolkit model.[4]

I created the Resilience Toolkit as a framework and process to help people develop an embodied understanding of their stress, trauma, and relaxation responses so they could discern when a response is adaptive and learn how to choose and use a set of real-time mindfulness and movement practices to settle excessive responses. As people grow their self-awareness, they better understand how trauma shows up for themselves and others in ways that impair their mental, emotional, and social functioning personally and professionally. Because the Toolkit centers the bidirectional relationship between the individual and their social-ecological environment, including systems of oppression, people reject the narratives that blame them for having legitimate responses to toxic, abusive, and neglectful circumstances. And yet, people can start to recognize when a legitimate response that is dialed up too high puts them in fight energy and the dismantling mode when instead a connecting and generative action is called for.

■ ■ ■

As I validated the advocate's anger at the plight of immigrant street vendors caught in a hostile ecosystem, he settled and remembered that I was on his team and that I had been brought in to create a culturally responsive educational program for the investigators. I was able to share that we were planning to use the Resilience Toolkit approach to help the investigators settle their own trauma responses as a first step toward an empathic understanding of the street vendors and building toward more equitable and humane permit enforcement. As I described how fight responses are connected to self-preservation and can lead to the dehumanization vendors had experienced, I gently made the connection to how the advocate's fight response had caused him to dehumanize the investigators, replicating the exact behavior he despised and compromising the allyship we needed to transform enforcement. The advocate slowly took it in and replied, "We need those sessions too. All of us."

■ ■ ■

Encouraging any organization or system to undertake deep transformative work like the eTIRO approach is difficult. Disintegrating into unfamiliar territory and remaking infrastructure, culture, and relationships take tremendous bandwidth, especially if the organization tries to do so while they are still providing uninterrupted care and services. Most systems can only tolerate adaptive and evolutionary models as they simultaneously navigate multiple constraints. As a transformational model, eTIRO is more palatable in that it works along pathways familiar to organizations and eases them into the depths of change.

For human service–focused organizations and systems, the high priority placed on values provides a natural entry point for eTIRO with its emphasis on six key principle clusters adapted from SAMHSA: safety; trustworthiness and transparency; peer support; collaboration and mutuality; voice, choice, and self-agency; and cultural humility. Healthcare, education, and social service organizations elevate these and similarly aligned values such as dignity, respect, and equity in their mission and communications. So, value-centered conversations are a familiar shared language. However, most leadership teams and workforce groups are painfully aware of how far reality falls short of their professed values, especially when staff is squeezed between funding and regulatory constraints on one side and immense end-user needs on the other. The opportunity to position eTIRO to reroot in an organization's stated values is appealing to many leaders when they begin to understand the potential alchemical resilience engenders for people to actually embody, rather than enforce, their values. As people get better at identifying and managing excessive stress responses, they tend to spend less time in the fight, dismantling energy, and more time in a building spirit, which is the natural home of eTIRO and most of the human service values.

Although systems change is an inherently complex multilevel process, it is usually easier for organizations to start at the level of the individual, often in a training or instructional context. eTIRO follows this familiar entry point by grounding leadership and staff first in the Resilience Toolkit through short courses. Because we know that didactic education alone does not produce attitudinal and behavioral change, we have structured these courses to be interactive and experiential. Ongoing regular groups provide leaders and staff with the opportunity to collectively nurture their individual and shared awareness and resilience skills, which in turn make it easier for them to embody the eTIRO values and enact change through structured implementation processes.

eTIRO implementation occurs through a phased process that harnesses individual alchemical resilience into collective action. The foregrounding of the Resilience Toolkit training increases prerequisite change readiness. When people are more often in the building spirit, they have a greater sense of spaciousness and are more open to new ideas and ways of doing things. People have more energy and are more willing to spend it in change efforts, thereby increasing organization-wide buy-in. However, some leaders and staff will always be predisposed to change work and more inspired by the eTIRO model. Encouraging organizations to identify eTIRO champions early in the process is critical to a successful implementation. Ideally champions should be those with both formal and informal authority. Formal authority is associated with the ability to unlock resources by rerouting funding and allocating dedicated time and operational might. Informal authority brings the social capital needed to influence hearts and move feet.

Sometimes champions are spotted during the early phase resilience-building educational and/or practice sessions, but more commonly they arise in the second educational phase. This phase further builds change readiness through knowledge and skill development by anchoring leaders and staff in the eTIRO goals, principles, and strategic planning and implementation framework. Leaders and staff are guided while they explore the six key eTIRO principle clusters: safety; trustworthiness and transparency; peer support; collaboration and mutuality; voice, choice, and self-agency; and cultural humility. Through facilitated discussions, they envision what it would feel like if their organization centered these principles in policy and practice. The discussions humanize the members of the workforce to each other as they share what these principles mean to them both personally and professionally. People are often so energized by these embodied heart-centered discussions, that when they go on to explore where their organization is meeting or missing the mark, they become even more motivated for positive change.

At this point, people are ready to do a deep dive into the eTIRO goals: 1) to realize the widespread impact of trauma and understand potential paths for healing and liberation; 2) to recognize the mechanisms and manifestations of trauma and resilience in individuals, communities, organizations, and systems; 3) to fully integrate knowledge about trauma and resilience into policies, procedures, and practices; and 4) to actively foster healing and resist retraumatization. Each goal serves as an entry point from which people can learn more about the science and sociology of trauma, resilience, and healing. People are asked to reflect on how these concepts and experiences manifest in their own lives and those of the people they work with and serve. The interactive learning journey uses discussion, writing, and role play, making the material potent and evocative, which can often activate stress. This activation is not something to shy away from; rather, people can use it to build more alchemical resilience. At regular intervals, training participants are invited to drop into somatic awareness of their stress activation and draw on the Resilience Toolkit practices they learned in the first phase of capacity building. The participants learn that they have the ability to be with hard experiences and settle their systems so they can stay connected with their colleagues. The value of this embodied learning translates into growing self-trust in their capacity to successfully engage in eTIRO implementation.

■ ■ ■

Almost immediately during the investigator training it became apparent that the investigators were pawns in a system set up by politicians attempting to assuage angry business owners and NIMBY residents on one side, and fearful

and indignant vendors and advocates on the other. City officials had cre-
ated a complaint system and a set of laws to satisfy the business owners and
residents who wanted their neighborhoods free of vendors, but these same
officials promised vendors and advocates that the laws would not be fully
enforced. The investigators had no formal power to change the laws or to
challenge the political hierarchy. In their frustration, they were bitter and
apathetic, even, at times, toward their own colleagues.

Through the training's emphasis on embodied resilience, the investigators
began to settle and recognize the harm in their own stress responses. They were
better able to connect to each other, and through focused empathy-building
activities, they realized that all the stakeholders in the street vending program
had similar needs for safety, respect, and dignity. They connected their own
helplessness with that of the vendors. By the end of the six-session training,
the investigators were strategizing about ideas to increase multi-stakeholder
engagement in remaking the entire street vendor program. In the field, some
reported that they were able to use Resilience Toolkit techniques to settle their
own stress and have calmer interactions with vendors. The promise of eTIRO
was not fully realized, however, because investigator leadership lacked engage-
ment and was unable to implement change efforts throughout the organization
and out into the entire ecosystem. Had there been an opportunity to engage
leadership and provide similar training to each stakeholder group, there would
have been real potential for systems-level policy change that centered the safety,
dignity, and self-agency that the street vendor advocates wanted from the start.

. . .

Even if the lion's share of the work starts with the identified champions,
it is important to provide all leaders and staff with a blueprint for strategic eTIRO implementation. First, ensure that the eTIRO goals align with
the organization's strategic plan to provide a more durable connection
to funding priorities and energetic resource allocation. Then, to avoid
people feeling overwhelmed, encourage the organization to prioritize
starting the implementation by convening workgroups that focus on no

more than three of the ten possible domains of implementation. These include leadership and governance; policies and procedures; training and workforce development; screening, assessment, and service delivery; financing; physical environment; engagement and involvement; media and marketing; progress and results monitoring; and cross-system collaboration.[5] Eventually all domains will be thoroughly overhauled, but selecting some soft spots to begin with eases the workload.

The strategic eTIRO implementation is similar to conventional organizational development through iterative cycles of assessment, objective setting, action plan deployment, and results evaluation. Part of what sets the eTIRO approach apart is the micro-integration of the key principle clusters in all steps of the process. How things are done cannot be separated from the desired outcomes, and each action provides an opportunity to weave eTIRO principles more deeply into the relational fabric of the organizational culture. For example, if the prioritized domain is policies and procedures, what might change if collaboration, voice, transparency, and safety are centered? There would be a greater effort to make sure all impacted stakeholders were represented in the workgroups focused on each implementation domain, including groups like students, patients, and clients who are traditionally excluded from policy decisions. It is also more likely that there would be participatory decision-making processes within the meetings and transparent sharing of evolving policy discussions out to the whole organization and the people it serves. Threading embodied resilience practices into the meeting structure would help people recognize when their stress activation was pushing them too far into dismantling energy, and it would bring them back into more settled states in which they could more readily access the safety and trust foundational for authentic collaboration. The micro-integration of the eTIRO principles is transformative in and of itself as the culture shifts while working on the macro changes at the domain level.

As the organization works its way through each domain, workgroup by workgroup, the eTIRO implementation is bolstered by continually resourcing its champions through sufficient paid dedicated time for eTIRO work with a commensurate decrease in their regular non-eTIRO workload, as well as opportunities for professional and peer mentoring. Over time, as eTIRO becomes the default norm in systems and culture, the organization's need for champions decreases. Still, process improvement provides the organization with ongoing opportunities to deepen commitment to the key principles and assess how well it is meeting the eTIRO goals; the organization can both celebrate progress and address the oppressive and traumatizing relics it still has left to uproot. Now individuals fluidly move and collaborate, navigate the needs to build or dismantle as the occasion warrants, and remake the systems into places where they thrive.

PRACTICES

4

FROM DETOX TO RECOVERY

How to Heal in a Toxic World

Kerri Kelly

Around the time of my political awakening, I broke my back. It was a horrific horse-riding accident that should have probably left me dead, if not severely immobilized. Instead, it just left me with a lifetime of chronic pain. Like many other things in my life, I assumed chronic pain was something to be overcome and fixed. But my pain, much like the guilt and shame that accompanied my many sites of privilege, wasn't something to be conquered. It was something to be felt.

As I learned to listen, my pain became a sort of protest, a signal that my body could no longer tolerate living a lie. That being implicated and impacted by a system of violence and oppression isn't just happening "out there"; it is also happening in me. I know now that a flare-up is never isolated and always a sensory (often debilitating) response to the violence and injustice that are happening around me. Like my physical injury, these sociopolitical pain points demanded to be felt. Despite what systems of power are selling us (i.e., a sense of false security, control, progress), there is no escape. As Dr. King reminds us, "We are all caught in an inescapable network of mutuality, tied into a single garment of destiny."[1]

Recovery would require a whole and rigorous detox, one that understands the truth of our enmeshment—that we are shaped by the external world and are, in turn, shaping the external world. It is how we confront the limiting stories and beliefs we have internalized and inherited from dominant systems, how we disrupt and release default behavioral and response patterns, how we challenge our attachment and addiction to the comforts promised by dominant culture, and how we practice new ways of being and doing.

It's the Water

Nothing is softer or more flexible than water, yet nothing can resist it.

—LAO TZU

One of the biggest misperceptions about white supremacy is that it's about bad people doing bad things. "But white supremacy is not the shark, it's the water," says spoken word poet Guante.[2] The water is the culture that shapes the many systems that determine our well-being—healthcare, housing, economy, education. But it is also the centuries of systemic disadvantage, discrimination, and violence that people of color have faced—and continue to face today. This water is difficult to see, particularly for white privileged people like me, because we are swimming in it, immersed in it, and benefiting from it. Which is precisely what keeps it (and other systems of domination) in power—its ability to remain invisible and elusive.

The water is culture. And not just any culture. The term *popular culture* often implies that it is neutral and natural based on the public's demand, preferences, and consumption, whereas the term *dominant culture* acknowledges that much of what we know as mainstream culture (norms, standards, beliefs, values, and narratives) is created and controlled by those who have power over systems, structures, media, and enforcement. Dominant culture is the outgrowth of the legacy of separation, supremacy, and scarcity that preceded and produced the logic of colonization, the system of slavery, and the extraction of capitalism.[3] Dominant culture is built on myths that have distorted Indigenous wisdom. And dominant culture is the manifestation of unresolved and unchecked collective trauma.

Like water and air, the nature of culture is slippery and fluid, often shapeshifting into whatever keeps the system in place. It is impossible to avoid, permeating every tissue and cell in our bodies. We are molded and manipulated by its force. Socialization is how we learn to swim in this water—it teaches us stereotypes, fosters comparison, normalizes oppression, and demands obedience. This operating system is always functioning in the background, informing our relationships, institutions, and culture. When the water is toxic, we become immersed in ideas of separation, scarcity, and supremacy that shape our bodies and minds and work against our personal and collective well-being. Ultimately, dominant culture becomes the frame through which we see and respond to the world.

The other thing dominant culture does is obscure oppression and encourage us not to acknowledge the horrors that are all around us. It teaches us to rationalize inequality and justify harm. It encourages us to fend for ourselves at the expense of others. It overwhelms us with information and confuses us with lies. It decides who is normal and worthy of well-being. And it does whatever is necessary to maintain the control and power of those at the top of the social hierarchy. Those of us oblivious to the water become its soldiers and captives at the same time, often unaware of how the very system we are defending is attacking us. And when we start to peel back the layers of myths and falsehoods, what we reveal is not just deep systemic inequity . . . but a whole lot of gaslighting. Entire industries are designed to blame the individual and then profit from it. It says if you're sick or suffering, it's your fault. As I wrote in *American Detox* (2022):

> *Dominant culture betrays us in the following ways: First, it convinces us that if we are sick, sad, and exhausted, that's our fault. It's not the economy or structural imbalances or systemic injustice, it's you. "The lexis of abuse and gaslighting is appropriate here," says journalist and*

screenwriter Laurie Penny. "If you are miserable or angry because your life is a constant struggle against privation or prejudice, the problem is always and only with you. Society is not mad or messed up. You are." The other thing it does is try to sell us individual solutions to what it tells us are individual problems (which they're not). Stressed out because you are juggling two jobs and raising kids? You should try meditation. Feeling powerless and depressed because you are out of work? There is a mantra for that. Suffering from the symptoms of your chronic disease? Gluten-free can fix that. Can't afford to go to yoga? Manifest abundance.[4]

Dominant culture blames and shames us into obedience. But no matter who we are, we also shape dominant culture even as it shapes us. Paulo Freire, the Brazilian educator and activist, believed that we create culture and culture creates us. "Cultural invasion is on the one hand an instrument of domination, and on the other, the result of domination."[5] This "invasion" is absorbed, processed, and expressed through the body. Thus, the body becomes the site of both healing and liberation.

There's No Escape

The true focus of revolutionary change is never merely the oppressive situations which we seek to escape, but that piece of the oppressor which is planted deep within each of us, and which knows only the oppressors' tactics, the oppressors' relationships.

—AUDRE LORDE, *Sister Outsider*

Born into a white, female, non-disabled body in a small suburb outside of Manhattan, I was predisposed to privilege. It was not a clean slate but a tilted one, already weighed down by a history of oppression. The path was already paved for me. I would grow up to be cisgender, straight, always striving to be thin and fit, a professional, all-American, material girl. Like an avatar, I would be programmed accordingly, trained to play my assigned roles and do my part. I learned the rules along the way—that if I was a good girl, a good student, a good athlete, a good Catholic, I would be rewarded on earth and in heaven; that "I run like a girl" even when I beat every boy in my class in sixth grade; that everything that I had was earned through hard work and merit; that success is winning at all costs, climbing the proverbial ladder, competing and conquering anything and anyone who gets in the way of my progress; that white was right and normal and everything else was "other." There was no escape from this training for me, but I've found that radical self-awareness and accountability can challenge it and poke holes in its convoluted logic.

In the quest to understand what roles we have been socialized to play, how we are affected by issues of oppression, and how we participate in maintaining them, we must begin by making an inventory of our social identities and understand how they operate in relationship to power, privilege, and oppression. This is not for the sake of reinforcing categories or hierarchies but so we can understand what's happening so we can be strategic about how we make the personal, relational, cultural, and systemic changes needed to bring forth balance and equity. Whether we like it or not, we are each born into a specific set of social identities related to the hierarchies of difference (gender, ethnicity, skin color, first language, age, ability, class, religion, sexual orientation, etc.), which predispose us to unequal roles in the dynamic system of oppression. It's not that these identities aren't real; it's that a history of assigned value and ranking has been conferred upon them. Anyone who does not fit into the category of white, cisgender, male, straight, able-bodied, and wealthy (which is most of us) is deemed wrong and therefore subject to the threat of dominance through violence, exploitation, punishment, and/or isolation.

Socialization is the process of inducting the individual into the social world. It is how we learn the norms, values, standards, and expectations of us within a group or whole society. It is not inherently bad. Socialization is how wisdom and resilience get passed down from generation to generation—how Indigenous and nondominant narratives, medicine, and culture have historically, and still presently, countered and resisted the backdrop of dominance. But it is also how we have inherited and internalized racism and other systems of oppression over hundreds of years. In this context, socialization becomes a systematic training of "how to be" in the dynamic systems of oppression. Powerful forces, including institutions, mass media, and technology, operate to influence and enforce our participation in the system. Bobbie Harro, sociologist and author of "The Cycle of Socialization," says that this cycle "'teaches' us how to play our roles in oppression, and how to revere the existing systems that shape our thinking, leading us to blame uncontrollable forces, other people, or ourselves for the existence of oppression."[6] This process, like culture itself, is consistent, circular, self-perpetuating, and often invisible in the way in which it lands on us and in us, though not equally. The impacts and implications of this cycle are felt differently and disproportionately depending on our social location.[7]

Our socialization begins before we are born with no choice on our part. Each of us comes into a world in which the mechanics, assumptions, rules, roles, and structures are already in place and functioning. The dominant system that determines what is normal, favored, resourced, and uplifted was built long before we existed. After birth, we begin to be socialized by the people we are most proximal to, the people who are entrusted with our care—parents, family, friends—all the adults who are raising us. And whether intentionally or not, they pass on the self-concepts and perceptions, the norms, and the rules we must follow, the roles we are taught to play, and our expectations for the future. Once we start to engage with more public spaces and structures, our socialization gets amplified, and the more systems we come into contact with, the more it is reinforced. Whether we are attending school or going to church, receiving childcare or being exposed to doctors/hospitals, playing on sports teams, or navigating the playground or different social groups, we quickly learn how to be in public, who to look up to and look down on, what rules to follow, what roles to play, what assumptions to make, what and who to believe.

It is during this phase that stereotypes are introduced and reinforced, woven through every structural thread of our culture, fed to us constantly through the barrage of media all around us. As we grow up, we start to develop agency and the ability to think for ourselves. But what makes that difficult are the enforcements in place to maintain the social structure and uphold the status quo. If you follow the rules, you are not only considered normal but are rewarded in the form of awards, status, privileges, and material benefits. However, if you contradict the norm, you might run into a very real cost of being deprived, ostracized, or punished. The impacts of this system of socialization are undeniable—record inequality, violence against marginalized groups, and health disparities . . . all of which stem from the assumptions upon which dominant society is built—like dualism, individualism, domination, colonialism, scarcity, and hierarchy.

But we are not just impacted externally.

The body bears the brunt of this socialization—metabolizing every-thing it encounters. We don't just act out our conditioning through performance, obedience, defense, and complicity. We internalize these beliefs and behaviors in ways seen and unseen until they become the default system through which we operate in the world. Whether consciously or not, we come to believe these limiting stories about who we are and what we are (or aren't) capable of. Making some bodies wrong and other bodies comply is what Christine Caldwell calls *somaticism*. Making "the perceived body" (as opposed to the body experienced from within) conform to rigid, arbitrary, and abusive norms created by those in dominant social groups is likely a factor in eating disorders, poor body image, the objectification and commodification of the body, obsessive interest in a particular appearance, persecution of disabled people, violence against gender nonconforming individuals, delegitimization of people of color, and the subjugation of women.[8]

Every time we talk about bodies, we bring assumptions rooted in histories and beliefs about what is normal and what isn't. Normal is the predominant context that we live in, always operating in the background of our systems and choices. It is a consummate shapeshifter, masking itself in scientific discovery, medical innovation, and even wellness trends—all for the sake of fixing what is deemed to be broken or different. All of this is backed by a system that assigns "value to people's bodies and minds based on societally constructed ideas of normalcy, productivity, desirability, intelligence, excellence, and fitness. These constructed ideas are deeply rooted in eugenics, anti-Blackness, misogyny, colonialism, imperialism, and capitalism."[9]

For me, disability wasn't in the chronic pain I experienced for years, nor was it in my inability to sit or stand or walk for long periods of time; in my not being able to carry bags while shopping or traveling; or in losing feeling and function in my right arm. It existed in all the places I couldn't go, all the activities I couldn't engage in. It existed in the marginalization I experienced for not being able to keep up, put out, and fit into the ableist American Dream. And it existed in my isolation. The privilege that I'd experienced for most of my life had not only oriented me to see access and convenience as normal, but it made invisible the experience that one in five Americans have when they're confronted by a system that is designed to ignore and exclude them. Disability is not located in the individual's body and mind but in the world. It is a construct: a product of a toxic culture that defines desirability in the form of beauty standards, performance, productivity, and obedience.

Thus, the body becomes the primary locus of social order and control. Not just a site of exploitation, domestication, and enslavement, but an instrument of social law and order. We live in a world where people are constantly telling others what they can or can't do with their bodies. We're shamed from every direction—lose weight, act professionally, dress appropriately. It is not just the private struggle with our inner critic; it is a public expression of how we judge each other and are perceived and policed by systems of power. From incarceration to disability violence to antiabortion laws to fat shaming, we are struggling to defend our fundamental right to bodily autonomy. People who are Black, Indigenous, People of Color (BIPOC), trans and nonbinary, women, and/or living in poverty are especially vulnerable to being objectified and governed by legislation, religious institutions, employers, family members, and culture. Messages of what bodies are supposed to look like and what we are supposed to do with them circulate in every aspect of our lives.

Through socialization comes surveillance. Carceral logic encourages us to blame the problem on the individual when harm occurs and then isolate, punish, and often stigmatize that individual and the community they are a part of. It is done in overt ways by the state and criminal system, but also in more subtle, indirect ways that normalize punitive responses and celebrate redemptive violence, like when a child misbehaves in school and is suspended (excluded and removed), or when someone says something that makes a colleague uncomfortable and is publicly shamed for it, or when neighbors report neighbors for things they don't agree with and by doing so risk their displacement or eviction, or when people are humiliated on social media. These examples contribute to a culture that normalizes punishment and isolation as a response to social problems. Instead of challenging assumptions and the systems they arise from, we are encouraged to react with blame, retaliation, and punishment. Our response is to remove them—the offender, the wrongful, the different, the rule breaker—distance ourselves, and make them different from the rest of us.

"The reality of American freedom is that it requires that many of us remain captive to preserve the illusion of freedom for all," says Jasmine Syedullah.[10] She's speaking to how we've had to be judge and jury to each other for not living up to the American ideal—for not being white enough, for not being American enough, for not being independent enough, and so on. This single story not only flattens our humanity but robs us of possibility. Understanding the cost of this mindset is essential to getting free from it.

We Are Compromised

We are deeply entangled in the very systems we are organizing to change. White supremacy, misogyny, ableism, classism, homophobia, and trans-phobia exist everywhere . . . We have all so thoroughly internalized the logics of oppression that if oppression were to end tomorrow, we would be likely to reproduce previous structures.

—MARIAME KABA, *WE DO THIS 'TIL WE FREE US*

In order to survive in the dominant paradigm, we must be willing to deny basic truths inherent to our human experience. Vanessa Machado de Oliveira Andreotti calls it *constitutive denial*—"what we need to forget in order to believe what modernity/coloniality wants us to believe in, and to desire what modernity/coloniality wants us to desire."[11] We deny things such as

- our complicity in the "systemic, historical, and ongoing violence" (that comes from our shared legacy of separation, supremacy, and scarcity);
- the "limits of the planet" (that the rate of extraction and consumption is unsustainable);
- our interdependence (that we are not separate from each other, from the land, and from all of life); and
- the gravity and complexity of the problems we are facing (that threatens our collective survival)—all of which compromise our ability to feel, relate, imagine, and create.[12]

These denials are not benign; rather, they are deeply malignant in how they drive some of the biggest threats to our collective well-being and survival, such as climate change, inequality, and threats to democracy. Examining the impact of these denials (and the complicity that stems from them) is essential to our recovery.

We are physically shaped by culture and socialization. It is not just behavioral or psychological; it is physiological in that it informs how we respond to stress—which, as we know, is connected to most of the systems in the body. This biology of safety—real or perceived—is deeply affecting our health and well-being, impacting our relationships and ability to work across lines of difference, and navigate our reality. And when we are too busy or disembodied to answer these questions for ourselves—"Am I safe?" "Do I belong?" "Do I matter?"—culture answers them for us. It tells us who is safe and who isn't, who gets to belong and who doesn't, whose lives matter and whose don't. Culture colludes with trauma to keep us stuck and scared.

Add to that a state of acceleration such as ours, exacerbated by a manufactured culture of fear, and the nervous system gets stuck in a chronic state of defense. Consider the socially acceptable ways we act out our trauma in the modern world—*fight* in how we're encouraged to blame/scapegoat and buy into the zero-sum paradigm that says for me to win you must lose, *flight* in how we're invited to escape through wellness and drugs, *freeze* in how immobilization gets expressed through apathy or not-my-problem politics, *appease* in all the ways we comply with systems of oppression, even protect and preserve it.

It's not enough to get educated and "change our minds." "If this were the problem, just giving people more and better information would correct their knowledge problem. But we don't just have a knowledge problem— we have a habit-of-being problem; the problem of whiteness is a problem of what we expect, our ways of being, bodily-ness, and how we understand ourselves as 'placed' in time," says Alexis Shotwell, author of *Against Purity: Living Ethically in Compromised Times.*[13] Shotwell argues that individual attempts at personal purity and perfectionism are not just impossible; they are also inadequate in responding to the overwhelming and complex issues we are facing. Yet so often our immediate reflex in the face of that which we cannot control collectively is to try to control it personally by perfecting and purifying our individual lives—if we just worked better or lived cleaner, we'd be able to arrive in a better place. To bring about less suffering and more thriving, we must accept complexity and imperfection as the natural basis of our lives. We are imperfect, imprinted by an unbearable past and unequal systems of power that are shaping our present reality. It does not matter how direct or indirect our engagement; we are embedded in it nonetheless.

Little has been done to study the neurobiological impacts of dominant culture on the brain and the body and the effects of our denial, compliance, and collusion with the violence and destruction that accompany it—like what happens in the brain when we feel superior to others; or how we are shaped by the conditional desires for more, for better, for control; or what neural pathways enable the tradeoff we make when we negotiate certain modern benefits in exchange for the violence and exploitation that accompany them; or how we unhook ourselves when we are being fed a chemical cocktail (through rewards, consumption, numbing, and entertainment) that keeps us attached and addicted to the false promises of the dominant culture. Recovery challenges us to consider not only the impacts and imprints of modernity but also our addiction and attachment to it.

Which brings us back to our bodies . . . as the sites of both harm and healing. The impacts and implications of the culture of dominance land on and in our bodies in different and disproportionate ways. People with the least proximity to power/privilege may experience deprivation and denial of resources, exclusion, exploitation, oppression, isolation, and shaming, whereas people with more proximity to power and privilege must reckon with the wound of complicity and collusion. The price of avoiding the pain associated with our complicity is that we become disembodied, unable to feel, and apathetic in the face of horrific suffering. In order to cash in on the privileges associated with dominant groups, people have had to fear, disown, demean, ignore, dehumanize, murder, incarcerate, and segregate ourselves from the majority of humanity, which begs the questions: What is the cost of our dependency on and attachment to the privileges of the dominant culture? How do we unhook ourselves from the dynamic cycle of privilege and oppression? Who are we beyond what dominant culture tells us we are? and What future is possible beyond modernity? This inquiry is alive in me, no longer just a momentary flare-up, but a chronic blaze that manifests in pain and anxiety and demands full attention and accountability.

Each time my body remembers, I am once again thrown from that horse, made aware of my defenselessness by the forces that encroach upon it. These imprints accumulate like badges, shaping me into the defended and suspicious person I have become. I carry them with me, like a passenger in a car. Wherever I go, my wounding comes with me; it helps me navigate danger and make sense of the world around me. It senses, before I do, the threat or injustice and moves to act. It is my irrational survivor and my fiercest advocate. No longer am I held hostage by the pain of my complicity, nor do I turn away from it; I choose instead to lean in.

Dissonance is most painful when it strikes at the heart of how we see ourselves. But when faced with the discomfort of contradiction that accompanies dominant systems and our place in them, we have a choice. We can either dig into denial and retreat to our individual bubbles or we can lean in and let ourselves be implicated and impacted by our shared humanity. Once we become aware of where and how we are situated inside the dynamic system of oppression and dominance, we can take responsibility for our part in this mess and lean into what lies beyond it.

Practicing Change

We have to live in a way that liberates the ancestors and future generations who are inside of us. Joy, peace, freedom, and harmony are not individual matters.

—THÍCH NHẤT HẠNH, *Fear: Essential Wisdom for Getting Through the Storm*

I'm reluctant to offer any prescriptions for how to detox and divest from dominant culture because that just seems like more of the same. And yet we must *do something*. To remain caught and compliant is only going to reproduce the conditions that got us here in the first place. As Kazu Haga noted in our Foreword, we'd do well by heeding Audre Lorde's caution that "the master's tools will never dismantle the master's house."[14] And while working inside systems and paradigms of dominance is often necessary to reduce harm and redistribute resources (especially for those of us who bear the least risk), this will never get us free. So, in this section I simply explore ways we can practice moving away from what is harming and holding us back and move toward that which is healing and expansive.

Practice is doing what is unfamiliar and uncomfortable over and over and over again. Unlike *habit*, which is a repetitive and unconscious behavior, practice is a deliberate and intentional action that moves us in the direction of who we want to be. To practice healing is to return to a relationship with one another and all of life. It is to know ourselves as essential parts of something bigger than us. It is to come undone, drop our shields, and question everything. And it is to detox from the ideologies of separation, supremacy, and scarcity so that we recover our lost selves and return to wholeness.

But practice does not look the same for everyone. Our different social locations affirm both our inherent connectedness and our diversity. While we are all whole humans, we are having a very different experience of being alive on the planet based on our different social locations. And we are impacted and implicated in very different and disproportionate ways. That means that healing and action are going to look different for each of us. adrienne maree brown reminds us,

> *If our ancestors did things to imbalance the scales, our work is to seek the balance available in our lifetimes. For some of us that means reparations, and for others it means reclamation. Because concepts such as race and nation are constructed with ever-changing boundaries and rules and power dynamics, most of us have to find some balance of both reparation and reclamation in how we move into accountability with our lineages, in what we allow to flow through us into the future.*[15]

Because we are entangled in all things, this invitation to practice is needed at the level of self (personal, individual), social (relationship, community), and system (institutions, systems, culture). As you explore this practice and pathway, it is essential to discern the map from the terrain. The map offers orientation and direction based on assumptions and intelligence. But the actual terrain—the unexpected and dynamic conditions we navigate on our way to liberation—can only be understood through engagement. Practice is the art of discipline, not control. It is not concerned with destinations so much as it is with the journey and the experience of moving through. Essential to this work is play and our ability to explore our right to freedom and what is possible beyond control and order. It is the willingness to experiment with that which has never been done before so that we can expand the capacity of who we are becoming and what is possible.

Practicing at the Level of System

Every crisis, actual or impending, needs to be viewed as an opportunity to bring about profound changes in our society. Going beyond protest organizing, visionary organizing begins by creating images and stories of the future that help us imagine and create alternatives to the existing system.

—GRACE LEE BOGGS, *The Next American Revolution*

While there is no escape from the complexity and trappings of modern life, we can continuously choose to disrupt and divest from violence, injustice, and unsustainability and reorient ourselves around cultures of care and mutuality.[16] This is particularly challenging at the level of institution/structure/culture where entire interlocking systems have been designed around expectations that put profits over people, extraction over living systems, individuals over the collective. For those of us working inside these institutions, it means holding the many contradictions that will emerge as we bridge and broker between old, expired ways of doing and new, experimental ways of being. As long as the water is toxic (poisoned by the white supremacist capitalist patriarchy), reforms and interventions (i.e., diversity, equity, and inclusion [DEI] work) *will be* imperfect and insufficient in transforming our systems and structures, but they are necessary in the short term for harm reduction and creating a more equitable present and future. For those of us working inside of institutions, here are some questions that might help move us in the direction of recovery:

- Is the institution willing to tell the truth about past and present harms, name the ways it is in collusion with toxic systems of injustice (like capitalism), and explore repair?

- How are patterns of power and dominance at work in our space?

- Is there a shared commitment to transform the structure/culture?

- Is there a culture of accountability that encourages responsibility and can hold a process of repair?

- Is there representation (and power to make change) at the margins?

- Is there a shared capacity for the conflict and change that will accompany this work?

- Is the process of equity (and all that comes with it, including disruption, speaking up, inviting accountability) valued and rewarded within the institution?

A necessary accompaniment to the practice of disrupting dominant patterns and paradigms is organizing ourselves and our systems around life-affirming values. Many of us are painfully aware of how toxic (dominant) culture has shaped our institutions (fostering competition, rewarding perfection, driving burnout, weaponizing scarcity, prioritizing outcomes over relationships, worshiping the bottom line). The question is: What values and priorities do we want to orient around as we build a better future for all? While it is important to understand what we are actively moving away from, it also matters that we know what we are actively practicing toward. This inquiry will require a radical reimagining of the future and conditions we need to create for everyone to thrive. It will challenge us to lean into uncharted territory and experiment with different ways of being and doing that can generate new possibilities for our shared future. And it will call us to choose, over and over again, life-affirming practices that celebrate everyone's value and wholeness.

From that place, we can organize. Organizing is how we get in shared alignment around what we need and value and build the power that is needed to bring that to fruition. For centuries, institutions have told people (especially marginalized people) that they don't have power, that they must settle for the status quo and accept the reality of an unequal world. But healing resistance organizer Kazu Haga reminds us that we have to "cut through the delusion that we are powerless" and realize that together we have the power to change our conditions.[17] Organizing is just that: it creates the conditions where more people have the power to resist and create systems that take care of everyone. When we remember that we are more powerful together, we can choose to show up for each other.

Practicing at the Level of Social

The lie of individualism is not just that we are separate exceptional selves, but that we can heal ourselves by ourselves. And yet everything around us is underlying our interdependence—from infectious disease to inequality to climate change. For us to survive and thrive, we must return to the deep knowing of our relationality. Recovery requires that we attend to the many breaks and severs brought about by the history and culture of dominance. Central to this shift is centering the sacredness of our relationship to each other and the world around us, where we are guided by our inherent dignity and understand ourselves as part of, not apart from, the living world.

Social fabric is sown one relationship at a time. It is how we build trust with one another in big and small ways. It is the courageous conversations that reveal the truth of who we are and who we are to each other. And it is the actions we take for the well-being of everyone. Community is an invitation to know ourselves in relationship with everyone and everything around us. It's where we practice showing up in our truth and being accountable to the whole. This means asking who needs to be in the room and what conversation needs to happen so that we can build deep threads of trust, relationship, and accountability that move us forward. It is in these exchanges that we get to practice showing up, being seen, learning in public, asking for what we need, doing repair work, and "putting our hearts on the line" for the sake of healing and transformation.[18] Here are some questions to guide our recovery:

- How do we disrupt cycles of harm and repair the wounds of our past?
- How do we work across lines of difference with understanding that we are impacted and implicated in different and disproportionate ways?
- How do our social locations inform how we show up in relationship and collaboration?
- What is our unique role and responsibility from where we stand in dynamic systems of oppression?
- How do we create the cultural conditions where accountability is practiced and repair is possible?
- How can we practice in real-time the future we are moving toward?

Practicing accountability is how we come back into community with one another. Accountability doesn't just right wrongs and repair relationships; it reveals the interlocking nature of our oppression and the mutuality of our liberation. While we all occupy different locations in this fucked up system of oppression, our survival requires all of us to show up in love and accountability for the future that we all deserve. It's not so much about being good as it is about doing less harm and living our way into a culture of accountability and mutuality. When I account for the harm I have done, the harm that I am a part of, I can begin to heal and repair the relationships that have been broken. When I get curious about how toxic beliefs and behaviors live inside of me, I can approach this work with humility and compassion for myself and everyone else who is trying to unlearn supremacy and imagine something better. I, like so many, am yearning for a world beyond what dominance has taught us about who is whole and human and worthy of well-being and who isn't.

Practicing at the Level of Self

Who am I really when so much of what I believed myself to be has been shaped by a culture that never wanted me to see beyond the veil?

—REV. ANGEL KYODO WILLIAMS, quoted by Kerri Kelly in *American Detox*

The self is inside and in between all these things. This makes our personal practice critical not just to our individual healing, but to our social, political, and ecological healing. Practice at the level of self looks different for different people depending on our lived experience and proximity to privilege and oppression, but for all of us, it involves radical awareness, action, and accountability. It starts with asking hard questions—questions that challenge and complicate our own truth and having some critical awareness around the stories we make up—fact-finding, and getting curious about what we are feeling. It's how we check ourselves and interrogate the stories that we tell ourselves about ourselves. This "interrogation" isn't about judgment or shame—those are just more weapons of division. Rather, it is a willingness to see ourselves clearly, to see how we have been socialized and shaped by a toxic culture, to see how we have become separated from the truth of our mutual belonging.

The nature of this practice is not so much about fixing or becoming, but about detoxing and recovering. Rev. angel Kyodo williams explains,

It is this willingness to keep being willing to come undone—to do what we can to understand the world around us and how we operate and what is impacting who we are and how we are, and to allow that to keep coming undone. That's what I think is really the paradox in what

is possible, from a liberatory standpoint, is to recognize, oh, we're not trying to become something, we're trying to un-become. We're trying to undo ourselves.[19]

The practice of unlearning invites us to question all that we have learned, to strip away the veils and delusions of dominant culture, to interrogate our attachments to the promises of comfort and convenience, and finally, to reckon with what it has cost us. From this place of spaciousness and freedom, we can choose to do something different and make ourselves available to imagine and respond to what is emerging in its place. Here are some questions to accompany this personal recovery:

- How can you stay awake to the world and present to what is real?
- How do you bring your/our bodies back into the conversation as vessels of wisdom and intelligence?
- What were you taught about what is normal, right, good, desirable, deserving and what isn't?
- How can you build a capacity for the discomfort, disorientation, and, often, failure that comes with this practice?
- What desires or attachments (to the benefits of dominant culture) might get in the way of your recovery?
- What do you need to grieve that is dying or no longer serving the collective?
- What do you need in order to practice love, accountability, forgiveness, and joy?

During this process, doors will close and we will have to open them again. We will forget ourselves and have to remind each other. We will make new mistakes, cause harm, and have to practice repair. We will face uncertainties and setbacks and have to dream bigger. But practice prepares us for this work; it helps us build capacity through rigor, humility, compassion, and joy. Thriving in the face of the many accelerating crises we are facing will demand a commitment and capacity that none of us can muster on our own. We will need the depth of our courage and the width of our connections if we are to stand a chance against extreme inequality, mutating virus pandemics, climate calamity, and mass migration. We must reach both inside and outside ourselves, across divides, beyond borders, and toward one another—not just to ensure our collective survival, but to realize our full potential.

5

ACCOUNTABILITY, FORGIVENESS, AND MOVING TOWARD ONE ANOTHER

Jacoby Ballard

In 2020, I supported two friends in two very different circumstances. Both had caused harm that tapped into collective wounds: one involved betrayal in a romantic relationship and the other involved being called out publicly for how white supremacy surfaced in their organizational structure. I was called to move toward each of them because I believe that when any of us create harm, we need and deserve support and attention, not isolation and shame. Both friends had been abandoned by countless people in their lives; I saw others erecting these sharp and immediate boundaries as an unexamined and unconscious intent to punish. Perhaps people saw my friends as perpetrators who should not be associated with, perhaps they thought their actions contagious, or perhaps the people in their lives thought disassociating with my friends would mean that they themselves were above or beyond the harm that had been created. Part of what was painful about each situation was how deep (and common) each of the wounds caused by my friends' behavior were. Many people have experienced dishonesty and betrayal in sexual or romantic relationships. Racialized wounds in our country from centuries of white supremacy impact any cross-racial relationship, and many organizations with white leadership and BIPOC staff have been called into question since 2020.

In these circumstances, I witnessed acute suffering piled on top of a deep cultural chronic pain. In each of these instances, my friends made mistakes or behaved in harmful manners and had relationships severed as a result; they faced significant online and in-person shaming; and the ruptures had an extended impact on their mental health, their sense of belonging, and their ability to meet their economic needs.

Rather than turn away as others had, I moved toward. I had the relationship (and therefore the necessary trust), and I had tools. I wasn't always like this, though. I had personally used the weapon of calling out in minor and private ways, especially during my over-five-year experience at the Third Root Community Health Center in Brooklyn. What turned me to calling in was a fairly quiet event—a South Asian yoga teacher was late to teach her scheduled class. Rather than approach her with curiosity and presume that something had happened to delay her rather than her being intentionally absent, I judged her and called her out. I was in a position of authority as a white business owner, and she was in a fairly tenuous position as an independent contractor. What I learned later when she had the courage to tell me was that her dad had had a stroke, which she had found out about that morning, and she was frozen by the experience, unable to communicate about her yoga class amid the gravity of the news. I felt ashamed for having judged her, threatening her employment, and I learned a deep lesson: there's always a reason.

I shifted, then, to calling in. To listening. To paying attention and moving toward one another when there is conflict, rather than building walls. To using misunderstanding, errors, conflict, and rupture as opportunities to deepen rather than abandon relationships. This course of action demands diligence, fortitude, curiosity, and assuming one's best intent while centering the impact of harm, honesty, vulnerability, and forgiveness. And I believe it's the best way to live into the liberated world that we imagine.

. . .

Harm is inevitable in our lives, even as we work to reduce it. Harm occurs in our movements for social justice, and, at this point, we are not so great at repair. The Buddhist understanding of suffering, or *dukkha*, includes everything from a paper cut to the multigenerational negative impact of an action. It's also important to understand the political context of *harm*— what replicates or reinforces systems of oppression is particularly painful to communities that are targeted by those systems. As Michelle Cassandra Johnson writes in *We Heal Together: Rituals and Practices for Building Community and Connection*, "The way we talk about harm is often determined by the context, who we perceive to have caused harm or hurt, who we perceive as having experienced harm, power dynamics and the influence of dominant culture in a specific context . . . I am always connecting harm with systems and systems of oppression."[1] Many of us have internalized the carceral model of shame, blame, punishment, and isolation as a response to harm, which doesn't create transformation or repair broken trust—rather, it sentences people to a life of great suffering. As adrienne maree brown reminds us, "There is a degree of loss and pain that is a part of the human experience, but we can heal our relations to each other to move toward a reality in which no one is given a life that only produces trauma and suffering."[2] We need to address harm in ways that don't cause our relations and movements to fracture or disintegrate, but rather to become stronger, bonded by trust, created through repair.

I feel called to put into conversation calls for accountability and timeless practices of forgiveness, encouraging their greater presence in our movements. I find calls for accountability to be much more present and to take up more space than practices of forgiveness. And I know that in order to have authentic forgiveness, we must make room to grieve our individual and collective errors and harmful habits. Forgiveness is an inner job— no one can demand it, expect it, or feel entitled to it; when that occurs, our armor goes up and we get defensive. And yet, to release the burden and move into true liberation, we must find the spiritual strength to forgive individually and collectively. The internal work of forgiveness and the external manifestation of repair have been some of the most powerful aspects of social justice work I have witnessed.

Calling Out versus Calling In

Let's begin by exploring the differences between *calling in* and *calling out*, a set of concepts and practices that may seem well known to many in social change work today but that still require further unpacking.[3] I put this forward as someone who relied on calling out for a decade, after which time I did enough self-love and forgiveness work to have the inner resources to call someone in. Calling out is easier and faster in some ways because it's not about giving and receiving feedback, accountability, or vulnerability. Calling in is demanding and a long-term investment because it is relational; it involves recognizing that harm happens relationally, and thus healing also occurs relationally, including healing from systems of oppression.

Calling out relies on shame, guilt, punishment, and blame to transform behavior. Let us note that these are the same methods used in the prison industrial complex. Calling out creates separation and isolation and severs relationships. It imagines one right way forward, rather than a multiplicity of ways. There is one singular direction of communication. The person who created harm is not invited to provide background or context. Calling out targets the person who created harm rather than the system that indoctrinates us all in systems of oppression—it is an individual's responsibility to think, speak, and act toward harmlessness and not replicate systems of oppression; it is not one individual's fault that they are replicating systems of oppression. We are only responsible for our own thoughts, words, and actions, not for the whole system. Calling out should only be used as an emergency brake, as adrienne maree brown suggests, when every other method has been attempted, every other tool engaged.[4]

Calling in, on the other hand, recognizes that we all have the seeds of love and the seeds of hatred within us, and our actions depend on what we (and the larger culture) water. Calling in relies on strong relationships to hold the harm and the associated guilt and shame with care and attention. Calling in imagines multiple pathways forward and involves listening to all involved. It is by now a social justice norm to center the impact of harmful words and actions, but we must not ignore the person's intent or the context of the behavior; that matters. Calling in invites curiosity, reckoning with one's own culpability in a situation, offering up vulnerability, and holding the gravity of the heartbreak. Calling in places blame on the system rather than the individual, while supporting individuals to uproot the systems of oppression that grow inside of each of us.

We may need to discharge our anger and heal separately before trust is a possibility again; affinity spaces (spaces held for BIPOC or women, for example) are powerful places to do this, places where certain microaggressions do not need to be navigated or where open wounds do not get scratched. The disappointment, betrayal, and impact of harm may need to be held and guided by trusted healers and beloveds, and then, perhaps, we can come back together again, unarmored and self-reflective. Discharging anger can involve physically or vocally moving the energy and urgency of the anger as a way to respect the wisdom it presents: that something is wrong and must be dealt with. Once the energy of anger is intentionally released, words can more easily be received and held.

I see calling out as a less mature response to harm. I see this in myself and in fellow movement people. I get it. There is a collective sense that violence is going down that must stop, and when you don't have a ton of tools in the toolbelt, an emergency brake seems like a good option. When you've been around for a few decades, you've been both a recipient of and a creator of harm. Seasoned organizers are humbled rather than self-righteous, softer than we once were (or, unfortunately, hardened by resentment that arises from refusing to forgive and move on).

Of course, there are situations in which it is skillful to use the emergency brake. Sometimes calling attention to something publicly is the only way to shift behavior, often when a person's public image matters to them more than their own internal sense of integrity. We saw this in the #MeToo movement: public callouts when other methods either failed or were not attempted. But we must be attentive. If a person's highest concern is the public image, how deep and lasting of a change are they going to make?

Boundaries, Affinity Groups, and Healing

Prentis Hemphill famously wrote that a good boundary is one in which "I can love you and still love myself." This approach to boundaries as an act of love has been deeply influential in my life, and it is one that our social justice movements are benefiting from. Hemphill offers further, "Boundaries give us the space to do the work of loving ourselves. They might be the first and fundamental expression of self-love. They also give us the space to love and witness others as they are, even those that have hurt us."[5]

We don't live in a world where boundaries are honored or respected. Many of us are not good at erecting them with grace or at halting our words and actions to respect someone else's boundary. Systems of oppression bulldoze boundaries, threatening individual and collective safety, dignity, and belonging. Thus, targeted people putting up boundaries is an act of self-love, and respecting those boundaries is an act of love across difference; honoring what someone says is required to heal.

> *Americans have reached a point of peril and possibility. We will either grow up or grow smaller. This trauma will either burst forth in an explosion of dirty pain or provide the necessary energy and heat for white Americans to move through clean pain and heal. Only this second outcome will provide us with genuine safety.*[6]

I think we can travel many more paths than these two options, but Resmaa Menakem wisely perceives the ends of a spectrum of this political moment. Menakem proposes that white-bodied Americans and Black Americans heal separately so that our nervous systems can settle and harmonize with people around us rather than being triggered by one another. This is the value in affinity groups—not only for communities targeted by systems of oppression, but also for those who benefit from those systems—to educate one another and transform together in spaces where the group that is targeted or that benefits from the system is not required to bear witness. This separation is not the ultimate place to land but is often a necessary step to get to collective healing.

Integrated spaces, where people with different identities and positionalities are present, are a potent practice ground and sacred space, too. It's a practice ground for people with privilege to show up in a different way, to not control the space and to pass leadership, to practice settling their nervous systems rather than gripping. For folks with privilege, it is an opportunity to act with consideration to requests made in the past and to gain an understanding of where wounds lie. Integrated spaces are a practice ground for targeted people to begin again, to try on trust, to believe the good intent even as we tend to the impact of someone's ignorance or the replicating of old wounds. There is always historical damage to contend with, yet the magical thing is that relationships across difference can be incredibly healing, both individually and collectively. So, we can approach them as a place of coalition; as described by Bernice Johnson Reagon in "Coalition Politics," coalition work "is some of the most dangerous work you can do. And you shouldn't be looking for comfort . . . if you feel the strain, you are doing some good work."[7]

Forgiveness as a Movement Tool

Each of us has been hurt. Each of us has hurt people. We are bound to make mistakes. It's allowable. It's inevitable. Especially in proximity:

with coworkers, with family, we are going to create hurt because we are human. Undoing inherited norms of harm takes great awareness, attention, and commitment.

We are all reckoning with institutionalized, interpersonal, and internalized harm, and so it's bound to be reproduced in our movements. Forgiveness is about how we respond to and heal from the violence that has happened, given that it never should have happened in the first place. We are invited to face the harm head on and use our tools of boundaries, accountability, and forgiveness, which invites the possibility to transform harm into a generative process that restores rather than further fractures relationships and communities.

Forgiveness involves vulnerability and nobility, courage and presence, and it moves on its own timeline; you can't force it. I set my intention on forgiveness, for if I cannot offer forgiveness in this moment, I hope to be able to offer it in the future. I incline my heart toward forgiveness. Forgiveness is different from condoning wrongs and different from reconciliation. It is the personal practice of release; it may never lead to reconciling with those who have hurt you or those you have hurt, but it could.

I am curious about what is possible if we lean in rather than turn away when something goes down. As my friend and colleague Susan Raffo told me during a particularly difficult year in a worker-owned cooperative I was a part of in Brooklyn, "This is the work. It's not a mistake or an accident. This is what you signed up for."

A core understanding of forgiveness is that everyone has a basic goodness in them, and we can connect on that holy ground. Hurt people hurt people—when someone is hurting in their own body/heart/soul, they hurt those around them. This compels me to do my healing work as an act of generosity toward those I share greatest proximity with (and beyond), and it allows me compassion when harm goes down—rather than blaming or shaming, I seek understanding. I ask: What underlies these words and actions? Are you doing okay?

Everything we do matters. Every thought, word, and action matters. What we do with our hurt matters. If we don't process it directly, it can end up coming out the side of our necks, unintentionally and carelessly, when we don't mean it to.

Impermanence also reinforces our forgiveness practice—things might be painful right now, but that pain will pass. My beloved uncle may be homophobic right now, but that thought pattern could shift. Reflecting on the ways in which each of us has learned to be more skillful, to move in greater and greater alignment with justice, encourages us to consider that possibility of growth in all those around us. There is no solidity. This too will change. And if it will change, can we forgive what has already happened so that we can move with a beginner's mind into the next moment?

Accountability

The idea of holding someone accountable who has created harm within social justice movements is often an attempt to control someone else. We can invite someone into accountability; in fact, most trusting, courageous, and intimate relationships across difference involve (and demand) accountability. We can create boundaries in the interest of self-preservation if someone's words and actions do not change. But we only have control over ourselves; we cannot control someone else.[8]

When we don't have control over someone in our social justice communities who makes a mistake, too often we rely on carceral methods of shame, isolation, and punishment, and we sometimes even introduce greater obstacles for that person to overcome in order to survive.[9] What is the impact of these tactics? Are we growing our movements? Are we building trust within our movements? I don't think employing these tactics allows us to build power; rather, it is a projection of the pain that we feel from chronic systemic injustice that we project onto an individual.

We cannot make someone acknowledge their actions or their impact. We can't make someone *feel* remorse. We can't make someone make something right or transform. This is up to the individual. Clearly, I think accountability and transformation are in the best interest of an individual and for us to make collective progress toward healing and justice. I can provide feedback to someone, and I can be vulnerable and share how thoughts, words, and actions impact me; but I can't make someone accountable to me if they don't want to be. When we try to force accountability, we risk not being seen as genuine, we risk not being committed, because we are demanding rather than offering, and that is only a one-way street. As Alicia Garza has suggested, we can mutually decide we are entering into an accountable relationship, but if there's not a previously existing relationship, accountability is forced.[10]

Being willing to be accountable ourselves is a different thing. We should seek that kind of responsibility and move toward it. We are asking others to assist us in our commitment to our values and to shed light on what we might be unaware of. We are listening to feedback and the impact of our actions. We are in relationship. When interviewed about her restorative justice work with Common Justice, Danielle Sered suggested, "Accountability is active. I have to acknowledge what I did. I have to acknowledge its impact on others. I have to express genuine remorse. I have to make things as right as possible, ideally as defined by those harmed. And I have to become someone who will never cause that harm ever again."[11]

Accountability is an offering that we can make toward justice, toward our relationships, but it cannot be forced by someone else. "The path to a future in which humans can be in an authentic and accountable peace with each other is fractal—we must be willing to practice authenticity and accountability at the small scale of ourselves and our lives, both in ourselves and in our immediate relationships."[12] So, when a politician says something harmful, who will lean in? When it's revealed that a movement leader isn't leading with integrity, can we move toward them? When our partners, our children, our comrades betray us, can we slow down and get curious? Each time conflict emerges, harm is enacted, or oppression is reproduced, we have an opportunity to heal, to practice authenticity and accountability, but it cannot be forced.

Community Accountability for Harm

Drawing on my understanding of interdependence, I invite us to consider the accountability of the community when harm goes down. If we are inseparable, if we belong to one another, if our lives are bound together, then something in the community breaks down when harm happens. We are overly focused on individual responsibility in this country; we must also consider collective responsibility.

In a Buddhist class I taught in a prison, I had a student who was incarcerated for selling drugs in his community to make up for the economic hardship created from working a low-wage job. I conducted a compassion practice in the class where everyone wrote down a great suffering in their life on a small piece of paper, folded it up, and put it in a basket. Then everyone drew a note illuminating someone else's suffering. Before we read the drawn pieces of paper, I had students hold the paper in their hands with attention and care, knowing that they held someone's suffering. We then read the paper in silence and did a brief compassion practice. Then, one by one, we read each suffering out loud, taking a breath between each reading. We held each harm with compassion, and then I allowed them space for reflection.

My students wrote about not attending their mother's funeral, not being at home to parent their child, being incarcerated for the rest of their lives, having killed a best friend, inheriting HIV during childbirth, and addiction. My student who had sold drugs raised his hand and said that he drew the paper that addiction was a great suffering. He said, "I didn't cause this man's addiction, but I undoubtedly contributed to someone else's." He looked around the classroom at the men grappling with addiction and recovery and said, "I'm so sorry."

He had written about this in a paper as well, sharing that his sale of heroin was the cause of his incarceration. He had sold heroin for "quick money" so that he could feed and tend to his family. My response to him acknowledged that the fault wasn't entirely his. Every institution that pays workers low wages, that leads their employees to look for other quick ways to bring in money, contributes to this issue. Anyone who makes drugs that lead to addiction contributes to this issue. Government divestment in poor Black and Brown communities leads to this issue. Overinvestment in police and military and underinvestment in health-care and education lead to this issue. My student made a decision to sell drugs in his desperation, risking incarceration. But the larger society risked my student and put him in this situation, and we were never put on trial nor found guilty.

I want to invite you, reader, to look at harm in your life and in the lives around you similarly, to see the interdependence and therefore the wide-spread culpability. When we abandon and isolate one another in instances of harm, we attempt to avoid our own responsibility for harm created and go on with our lives, while blame is loaded onto a singular individual. In my response to his paper, I told my student that we failed him. He should have had other options. Society should have invested in his well-being so that the desperation he felt never would have arisen.

Even Privileged People Are Not Throwaway People

Many of us inhabit identities that have been dismissed, disregarded, or have become targets of violence. I write this chapter in a year when there have been an unprecedented number of legislative attacks on LGBTQ communities—there have been 492 anti-trans and anti-queer bills in state legislatures as of June 2023.[13] Many of us know what it means to be thrown away. That may be what leads us to political work or spiritual practices: to change the existing reality that is creating so much harm. Alicia Garza suggests, "A lot of us find movement from being rejected. A lot of us find movement from being targeted. You know, of course we would have these fears . . . but if we're gonna transform things right, then we've gotta be able to face fear and make sense of it and translate it into something else besides categories of exclusion."[14]

And yet, I see a reflex in some justice organizers to similarly disregard and dismiss those who hold positions of privilege. Of course, it's complicated, because part of that reflex is self-protection and an assertion of a boundary—"I will not do emotional caretaking here." However, someone must care. We are social animals, we are interdependent creatures, and we have needs. We learn and grow from being called into community, not from being canceled out of it. Someone must catch the tears of white women. Someone must attend to the suffering of white men. Someone must hear the cries of straight and cisgender folks who may feel "replaced" by queer values and "alternative" family models.

It's not everyone's role to hear every cry or attend to the unheard voices of people with the most privilege, for that can replicate harm or overwhelm people impacted by that unrecognized privilege. That is important. However, it's a very valuable role for people with similar positions—for organized and trained wealthy people to listen to (and ultimately organize) other wealthy people into wealth redistribution and returning their wealth to the communities that it was taken from. For cisgender straight men trained in feminism and uprooting toxic masculinity to work with men accused of sexual violence to help change their thoughts, words, and actions. For white women trained in racial justice to move closer to the Beckys and the Karens. This is the very notion of "go get your people," which has been clearly instructed to countless groups of people with privilege by targeted communities with the interest of stopping harm.

Martin Luther King Jr. said that "a riot is the voice of the unheard."[15] We can surely understand that about the racial reckoning of the summer of 2020, but can we understand that also about the insurrection at the US Capitol in Washington, DC, in January 2021?

Alicia Garza, cofounder of Black Lives Matter, reflects, "The Right is SO good at belonging. They don't let you go. They do all kinds of things to make you feel seen. They validate why you're there; they help you make sense of who is responsible for your pain, and they give you something to do about it."[16] The Left, not so much. Privileged people (and directly impacted people who have interest and bandwidth) could make an immediate impact by providing an alternative to disaffected white folks that calls them into accountability, community, and justice.

Social Change through Relationship

Lasting social change is about relationship. Relationships across difference compel those with privilege to leverage their access to resources and networks on behalf of targeted communities and make the demands of those communities heard and understood. We've seen this throughout history in the civil rights movement, the feminist movement, the Black power movement, the gay liberation movement, the labor movement. That alliance and solidarity come from a place of love that arises out of relationship, where our hearts quiver in response to the pain that our beloveds experience.

In order to be in long-term relationships across difference, we have to do incredible healing work. adrienne maree brown suggests, "What begins as a wound in one person can move like a sharp knife through a friendship, romance, workplace, family, or community"; there is great risk to not doing the work to heal those wounds.[17] Those with privilege need to heal from the ignorance created by privilege, the shame and guilt from being protected by and from being the beneficiary of systems of oppression. We need to make great efforts to pay attention to what is happening to other communities and to confront all the ways that we've internalized systems of oppression in small and profound ways. And those who are targeted need to begin to practice discernment and setting boundaries, to be open and curious to connection and relationship across difference, while not putting themselves in harm's way and not burning potential bridges. It takes a lot of healing work to become clear on what is a threat and what is not, what is intentional maliciousness and what is an ignorant and accidental reenactment of systems of power, when a historical wound got rubbed but not reinflicted. I believe that loving kindness and forgiveness practices are essential ingredients for all of us to heal enough to be in loving relationships across difference.

If I'm transforming myself, then people I'm in relationship with are necessarily pulled along in changing, too. If I am becoming more generous over time, healing from capitalist greed and the idea of hoarding resources and opportunities for myself, then my communities are becoming more generous as well. As I live in greater integrity to my commitments, then some relationships inevitably fall away, and some are bolstered. As we demonstrate and speak about our own growth, those around us take note.

If we don't have relationships across difference, then our hearts are not compelled to change. If you are able-bodied and don't know a single disabled person, then you may not think about that community as an incredible source of wisdom when a pandemic strikes. If you are cisgender and don't know a single trans person, then it's easy to pass bills barring us from sports and bathrooms—you don't know the pain that you're inflicting. If you are a born citizen of a country and don't know people who immigrated, are refugees, or are undocumented, you don't know the risk of deportation in picking up your child from daycare or seeking necessary medical care and other daily stresses that undocumented folks face. But when we know people and love people across differences, our thoughts, words, and actions change. They have to, or else the relationships break, along with our hearts. This is a slower method of social change, but it is lasting, because it is about our families, our neighborhoods, our communities.

■ ■ ■

My friends that I moved toward in 2020 are doing well; they have done some repair where there was rupture, some letting go of what and whom they cannot control, and they have shifted their lives in meaningful ways that may not have come about otherwise. They are both taking tender intentional care of their relationships, grounding in practice, and slowing down. For those who remained close to them, their transformations are beacons of hope. Our relationships have deepened. They have listened to critical feedback that I gave; they have even requested it, because they trust my kindness and integrity. They know I am not interested in punishment, but in us all living well in our places, as a process of becoming. They call upon my support in other complicated relationships, where matters of suicide, elder care, reproductive labor, and gender dynamics are on the table. They each have become discerning in which relationships are important to them and are committed to tending to and showing up for the relationships that they hold dear.

Shifting away from calling out to calling in, working with forgiveness, and offering and expecting accountability (but not demanding it) are all ways we can grow our social justice movements to have greater trust, become larger, and have greater impact. Our movements are only as strong as our relationships, so can we strengthen our relationship toolbelts out of devotion to social change? If our movements are grounded in trust, they are less permeable to obstruction and surveillance from outside actors, and we win greater and greater victories because we are not distracted by the latest calling out or the latest movement fracture. As disability justice organization Sins Invalid proclaims, "We move together."[18] May that be an invitation and a commitment for us all.

6

TENDING TO A BROKEN AND BRUISED WORLD

Centering Compassion, Loving Kindness, Joy, and Equanimity

Leslie Booker

I am writing this from my ink-blue corduroy couch in the living room of my home. This home is located on the territory of the Lenape people, who beautifully stewarded and continue to steward this land—colloquially known as West Philly. I'm not offering this land acknowledgment to let you know that *I* know about the Lenape people, but to remind me on a daily basis of what happens when we allow greed, hatred, and delusion to colonize our hearts and minds. Collectively known as the three poisons, these mind states create confusion and chaos, separating us and leading us to believe that we don't belong to each other.

I have many ancestors of liberation, but I specifically want to lift up Nani Bala Barua here, who was lovingly known as Dipa Ma—the mother of Dipa. As a young widow who was dying of a broken heart in the late 1950s in Bangladesh, she was prescribed meditation to save her life. As a single mom, she didn't have the luxury of spending hours on her meditation cushion or going away for months at a time for silent meditation retreats. So she found a way to integrate these practices of liberation into her daily chores as a householder, inspiring and encouraging other women to begin spiritual training as a practice in everyday life, which was unheard of at that time and is still radical in some spaces. By the late 1970s, she had become a great teacher to many young, white, American seekers, and she authorized a few to come back to America to share what would be useful to a society that was so broken. I was a very young child when this was all going down, and I wouldn't know about Dipa Ma, meditation, or the way out of suffering for a few more decades. Forty years later, it is this spiritual training as a practice in everyday life that has allowed these practices to be alive and relevant for my life. They enable me to navigate depression, injustice, and heartache with compassion, loving kindness, joy, equanimity—and a healthy dose of righteous rage.

Origin Story

I was nine years old when I witnessed folks experiencing homelessness for the first time. My sister and I were in the backseat of our parents' yellow Volvo as they drove us through the streets of Washington, DC, on a rainy afternoon. We had just moved back to the States after living in Japan for three years. Because we had left when I was five and a half, I didn't have a strong memory of the United States outside of my family of origin. I remember looking out the window of that backseat, trying to learn about my new home. What I saw were houseless people shuffling around, wearing dirty and ripped clothing. I remember being acutely aware that something wasn't right or just with this situation. This was one of my first conscious memories of the US. I developed a stutter after that moment that would last for a year; the ghost of it lingers when I'm angry and overly fatigued.

This was my first heartbreak.

It woke me up and shook me out of the comfort and safety of the brown interior of this yellow Volvo with its pioneering seatbelts in the backseats. The visceral memory of that experience is one of my quivering heart, which I would learn later was the embodied response to compassion.

I didn't grow up with an explicit teaching on compassion or knowing my own capacity for compassion. After experiencing that first quivering of the heart as a child, my next step was to be engulfed in rage. I was enraged seeing folks dismissed, ignored, not valued, or mistreated in our society because of their race, class, or gender expression; because they were living with the disease of addiction, fragile mental health, or were unhoused. My compassion almost immediately turned into anger that manifested as yelling, shutting down, and refusing to be in any kind of relationship with those I deemed "the enemy." I became a young and untethered activist, utilizing "the performance principle without the headache of accountability."[1]

As I grew to engage with multiple spheres of social justice activism, service, education, and organizing, I didn't know what to do with this fire, and so I allowed it to burn me up and slump me into deep depression for years. It wasn't until I came to my study of Buddhist philosophy and meditation practice many years later that I learned that fire was not meant to burn out of control—it was meant to act as a catalyst to *feel*, to get curious, and to move toward an understanding of my anger and what I was standing *for*, instead of what I was fighting against.

This chapter is about learning how to stand up for what you're *for* and how to *stay*. How to stay to bear witness; to stay when you're completely heartbroken or enraged; to stay in the midst of the chaos of a world on fire. It is about how we learn to embody nobility and dignity (from the Latin *dignitas*, which means worth or value). When dignity is facing out, it looks like me recognizing you as an extension of my own heart. I'll be sharing the Buddhist framework of the *four Brahmaviharas*, or heart practices, that have helped lead me there.

The Brahmaviharas

The word *Brahmavihara* is made up of two words: *Brahma* and *vihara*. Brahma is from the Brahmin caste system,[2] named after the god Brahma, also known as "the Creator." The folks who were historically designated as members of this caste were priests, royals, and spiritual educators. Vihara means home or abode. So together they mean "divine abode" or "heavenly abode"; the best home, the place where we rest our hearts. These four heart practices of the Brahmaviharas soften the edges without dulling; they can be a refuge for a weary mind or a rageful heart, and they remind us that we belong to each other.

I like to think of these four as a family of sisters; they all look really similar, but it's not until you line them up side by side that you begin to notice that one sister's hair has a bit more red in it, or another has a slightly curlier hair texture or freckles. Their Brahmaviharas' names in *Pali* (the language that the Buddha's canon of oral tradition was translated into) are *Metta, Karuna, Mudita,* and *Upekkha.* Metta is often translated into English as loving kindness, friendliness, or benevolence for all beings. Karuna, or compassion, starts with a quivering of the heart, asking us to start with an experience that considers another. Mudita, or joy, is not just joy for ourselves, but joy for another being's happiness and success. And finally, Upekkha, or equanimity, is the practice of a balanced heart and mind. Equanimity protects the heart in loving kindness from going into envy, protects compassion from sliding into what some call compassion fatigue, and protects the excitement of joy from becoming agitated. Because equanimity is a heart that looks through the lens of wisdom, it protects itself from being cold and apathetic.

As a meditator, closing my eyes and going inward hasn't always been the best medicine. For those of us who live with depression, anxiety, or other mental health conditions, sometimes silent meditation practice can exacerbate these conditions, especially when practiced in isolation and without guidance. And so, I'm happy to inform you that, though these practices can be cultivated with more depth while meditating, they are most easily practiced in daily life and in relationship with another— especially those that we find difficult to be with. And sometimes, that someone might be ourselves . . .

Compassion

Karuna: Near enemy—pity; far enemy—cruelty

Though the list of Brahmaviharas typically starts with Metta, my work through the heart practices began with *compassion*—this quivering of the heart that calls us into action. Oftentimes compassion gets conflated or mashed up with things that look, sound, and maybe even feel similar. These are called the near enemy of compassion, like pity or empathy. A good way to parse these apart is to imagine you've witnessed someone walk into a glass door.

Pity says, "Damn, that sucks!" and leans more toward the energy of having sorrow for another . . . and kinda stops there. Empathy, on the other hand, says, "Ouch, I *know* that had to hurt!" and again, stops there.

Compassion, however, is a two-part experience of first feeling empathy, and then moving toward the action of wiping the blood off the person's forehead.

Like most things, compassion is not a monolith, meaning that not everyone's expression of compassion is the same. It moves and shifts and transforms into the kind of compassion that is the appropriate response for what's needed. Sometimes that appropriate response is turning inward to first acknowledge and then create the space to honor and mourn what we have lost. Sometimes the appropriate response could be to hit the streets to reclaim our freedoms. Whatever our expression of compassion is, it is an act of love to pay attention to this energy of the heart, to turn toward it and respond.

Writer Toni Morrison said: "I know the world is bruised and bleeding. And though it is important not to ignore its pain, it is also critical to refuse to succumb to its malevolence. Like failure, chaos contains information that can lead to knowledge, even wisdom. That is how civilizations heal."[3]

Theravada Buddhist Monk Nyanaponika Thera says,

It is compassion that removes the heavy bar, opens the door to freedom, makes the narrow heart as wide as the world. Compassion takes away

119

*from the heart the inert weight, the paralyzing heaviness; it gives wings
to those who cling to the lowlands of self. Through compassion the fact
of suffering remains vividly present to our mind, even at times when we
personally are free from it. It gives us the rich experience of suffering,
thus strengthening us to meet it prepared, when it does befall us.*[4]

So, compassion is asking us to keep turning toward it; when we do,
we build up our resiliency and resistance to be with our own discomfort,
recognize our own pain, and connect with our own vulnerability. And in
turn, we are able to recognize and feel that in others.

My brilliant friend Teo Drake once said, "If you can move towards
your discomfort, I can move away from my pain, so let's meet somewhere
in the middle."[5]

Compassion does not condone bad behavior. Instead, it allows me to
see where a person got dropped along the way. As has been stated, hurt
people hurt people. And so, instead of meeting people's violence with my
violence, I pause to reflect on what could have made this kind of hatred. I
know that if I allow my hatred to match their hatred, then they have won.
I have allowed this poison to colonize my heart, to occupy space that I had
reserved for love and caring for my community.

bell hooks teaches: "For me, compassion and forgiveness are always
linked: how do we hold people accountable for wrongdoing and yet at the
same time remain in touch with their humanity enough to believe in their
capacity to be transformed."[6]

Like most things in life, this practice of compassion can be misun-
derstood and weaponized to justify all kinds of naughty and destructive
behavior. For example, a lot of us would benefit greatly from practicing
self-compassion: giving ourselves the same kindness and care we'd give to
a good friend.[7] And yet some folks, typically folks who dive into the deep
end of guilt and shame when they unintentionally perpetuate oppression,
can spiritually bypass taking responsibility for their actions in order to
practice self-compassion. There's a "yes, and" that needs to happen here.

Yes, it does not serve any of us to cower in the presence of our ignorance. Let's not turn away from this beautiful opportunity to be in relation with another, to learn something new, and to take this knowledge back to educate our communities. Again, Dear Ones, we belong to each other.

The manifestation of a far enemy of compassion (something that holds the opposite qualities) is cruelty, which has many faces. In this case, it takes the shape of disproportionality. As defined by Maurice Mitchell,

> *disproportionality can be a byproduct of uneven training on concepts like power and power analysis as well as a misunderstanding of strategy. This tendency ultimately weakens meaning, dulls analysis, and robs us of the ability to acknowledge and process instances of violence and oppression. If everything is "violent," nothing really is. If every slight is "oppression," nothing is.*[8]

So, Dear Ones, compassion is not meant to be a destination, but a continual practice of being able to see ourselves in others. It allows us to be inquisitive and curious instead of judging a person based on a small and broken-off piece of the potential of their humanity. Listening to this quivering of the heart is a movement toward a shared world.

Loving Kindness | Goodwill | Benevolence

Metta: Near enemy—attachment; far enemy—hatred

When people would ask that ridiculous question that all adults ask of children, "What do you want to be when you grow up?" I would say proudly and confidently, "I want to be a professional volunteer!"

What I was actually saying was, "I don't believe that the US government knows how to take care of its people and clearly there isn't a profession that I could engage in that would allow me to witness and support the dignity of all Beings."

But I made a promise to my nine-year-old self to find a way not to "help" folks, in that Sally Struthers sort of way that pulled at our heartstrings and demonstrated the near enemy of pity at its best, but to walk beside folks, and to share in their humanity.

For me to speak of Metta—this practice of goodwill, benevolence, even loving kindness, I have to start with its far enemy, hatred—which is a dear friend of one of my favorite emotions, anger.

When I was younger, I loved my unbound and unpredictable anger. It made me feel alive and strong, and sexy and powerful. I had my eyes closed, my ears shut, and my mouth wide open. I thought to be engaged with the world, you had to be bigger, louder, and angrier than everybody else . . . which almost immediately turned into burnout.

Maya Angelou wisely teaches:

If you're not angry, you're either a stone . . . or you're too sick to be angry. You should be angry! Now mind you, there's a difference. You must not be bitter and let me show you why: Bitterness is like cancer. It eats upon the host; it doesn't do anything to the object of its displeasure. So, use that anger, yes. You write it, you paint it, you dance it, you march it, you vote it, you do everything about it . . . , you talk it, never stop talking it.[9]

Now that doesn't mean pushing anger aside, not acknowledging it, or spiritually bypassing it. It means to be awake, alive, and to pay attention to what's happening around us, which brings us in direct relationship with incredibly strong emotions like rage and fear. To feel these things is an appropriate response to all the atrocities that we face in our day-to-day lives: the global pandemic, food instability, the impact of multiple climate catastrophes, xenophobia, homophobia, paternalism, and racism. We have the opportunity to influence and inspire the world in which we live. But we also tend to lean toward depression and collapse.

Thanissara, a former nun of the Insight tradition, shares that "anger untransformed burns us up, injures others, or more commonly, because we repress it, saps our life force and collapses us into depression."[10]

I experienced all of that. When I wasn't high off the adrenaline of my anger, I was deeply depressed. This tightness and rigidity was around my heart, and I experienced it as one solid mass that I had to push out of my body. I didn't yet understand that I could get curious about my anger, investigate it, feel where it started. I didn't know that it wasn't just anger—it was fear, and sadness, and grief, and a feeling of unproductivity while trying to move this big mound of injustice and inhumanity out of the way.

When I got curious about my anger, I was able to understand that it had a temperature, a viscosity, a texture; that it moved, that it shape-shifted, that it was impermanent. I could hang out with it for a while and understand that this anger wasn't all mine! I came to understand that some of our anger, especially the anger that feels too big for our bodies, can be the epigenetic inheritance from our ancestors who were rounded up and placed into holocaust and internment camps, our ancestors who were indentured servants, our ancestors who were enslaved, and all other forms of oppression that tried to destroy them.

I had to decide what was mine and what to do with it; how to honor it and how to transform it as a form of protection.

I eventually found my way toward a livelihood as a Buddhist philosophy and meditation teacher in the Insight tradition, a Western convert Buddhist lineage inspired by the Thai Forest monastics. In this work, I lead retreats and share *Dharma talks*—a sharing of the wisdom of the Buddha's teachings.

One of the first Dharma talks I wrote was called "I Fucking Hate Metta!" Not because I'm a monster or couldn't feel the impact of this practice of loving kindness and benevolence, but because I, like most folks who have a meditation practice, had learned Metta as a concentration practice; this systematic form uses these four phrases: may I be happy, may I be healthy, may I be safe, and may I live with ease.

The phrases start with wishing them to yourself, and then you move on and offer them to the next category of benefactor, a neutral person, and then a difficult person.

This practice was hard for me because, as someone who lives with a touch of neurodiversity, I simply couldn't remember the phrases! They would get all jumbled up in my head while I was trying to figure out which of my benefactors, neutral folks, and difficult people to add in . . . I would spend the whole practice in my head and not in my heart.

Another block on my path to centering my heart came when I shared these practices with the vulnerable folks I practiced with at the time; it was hard to say,

"May you be happy" to a kid who was locked up and away from their family;

"May you be healthy" to folks who were living with HIV and AIDS;

"May you be safe" to someone who was unhoused; and

"May you live with ease" to someone who was detoxing from addiction.

The near enemy of Metta is attachment: attachment to the outcome— to everyone being happy, healthy, safe, and having ease in their lives. Practiced in this way is not the practice of Metta; this is the practice of wishing for things to be different from what they are.

But then I heard a story from the Buddha's time about how he instructed the monks who were traveling with him to use this practice as one of protection. The story goes that they were traveling together, and the Buddha asked the monks to go and meditate in the forest. The tree devas (celestial beings) were not down with these new visitors and began to give off terrible smells and scary noises to scare the monks out of the forest. They reported this back to the Buddha and he offered them the teaching of Metta to take back to protect them. The legend has it that the tree devas were so moved by these teachings that they allowed them to stay.

In 2011, some friends and I cofounded the Meditation Working Group of Occupy Wall Street in New York. Every day at 3 p.m. we would gather around the Tree of Life at the northwest corner of Zuccotti Park to offer a meditation. Because we were a rotation of folks holding this space, we decided that we would use the practice of Metta for consistency. The years I had spent sharing this practice with young people whose wings had been clipped by the carceral system had trained me to keep my eyes open while leading meditations, in order to observe how folks were responding through their body language so that I could be responsive with my guidance. I remember one day observing the crowd of seventy-five people who were participating in our daily meditation: a mixture of Occupiers, tourists, and of course, some police on guard. As the meditation continued, I began to feel a shift around us; the tourists began to put their cameras down, and the cops took their hands off their guns and softened their postures. I let go of the words myself and began to drop into the felt sense of my body that felt "abundant, exalted, immeasurable, without hostility and without ill-will"—the impact of the practice of Metta.[11]

When I paid attention, I understood that this was available to me all the time, and I became curious about what was possible when living life with this practice, not just as an antidote when the heart shuts down or becomes aversive, but as my foundation for how I wanted to show up in the world. And when I was practicing this way—shedding the words, but staying with the felt sense in the body—the practice of Metta went from, as one of my students says, "undermining my practice to being the underpinning of my practice." This allowed me to open my heart a bit more and to be with the complexity of being human.

Sympathetic or Appreciative Joy |
Joy at the Good Fortune of Others

Mudita: Near enemy—comparison, hypocrisy, insincerity, joy for others, but tinged with identification (my team, my child); far enemy—envy

Mudita or appreciative joy is often described as the joy for another's happiness and success. Mudita is not a cultivation practice, meaning we don't have to go looking for it or utilize phrases to incline our hearts and minds toward it. This kind of joy is primordial. It's already living in our bodies—just under our skin. It lives so close to us, and yet it's incredibly challenging for many of us to know it, find it, feel it, access it, and experience it.

Most of us live in communities suffering from dominant culture supremacy: a culture that values power hoarding and power over, as opposed to power with or flat leadership, a culture that supports individualism instead of collective liberation; and this "either / or" thinking, which makes us believe that if something good happens for another person, then it can't possibly also happen for us.

Whenever I thought of having joy for another's happiness, for another's gain, it was always tinged with *just a touch* of envy. Ahh, the near enemy, the thing that masquerades as joy, but has an edge. And that nagging little comparing mind that says, "*Mine* is shinier than *yours*, and *mine* has glitter!" This near enemy is enshrined in comparison, identification, and individuation. For many of us, we can only be happy for someone if we know we're doing a little bit better than they are.

This is in the water we drink, the air that we breathe, and in so many implicit and explicit lessons we've learned along the way from our families of origin and dominant culture socialization. And so, it seems almost counterculture to live with a heart that is turned toward caring for another, and especially counter to bring our joy for another's success to the forefront of how we move through the world.

A divine experience of joy sounds like it would be full of laughter and exhilarated states, but that kind of performative exuberance is considered another near enemy or imposter of joy. In a retreat I was leading on these four heart practices, I asked folks what they had learned about joy in their upbringing, whether it was from their family of origin, their culture, their socioeconomic location, or somewhere else. Someone responded to this by saying, "My joy had been contaminated"; and the room began to unburden this heavy load. Many folks spoke to how they only knew or expressed joy if they had achieved or accomplished something, so joy was connected to striving, to being competitive. Another indicated that their joy had been attached to partying for so long, that their natural way of being in the world had been squashed or hidden. They learned that they weren't enough without intoxicating the body. Others said that things that brought them joy, like dancing and moving their bodies, had gotten deeply entangled with losing weight and a distortion of their body image. Some hadn't been able to go near their joy but now they were beginning to allow it to sit next to them on their meditation cushion. And some, bringing equanimity in, experienced their joy as a companion to their grief and sorrow.

The late author and educator Eileen Siriwardhana writes about how we, as a culture, can nurture sympathetic joy by recognizing and admiring the good that we see.[12] Because we live in a negative-biased culture, she presents Dorothy Law Nolte's classic poem that begins by showing us the impact of living in a hostile world and then shows us how we can cultivate qualities of care. Feel free to replace *child* with *my coworker, that annoying intern,* or *my aggressive boss,* and see if the heart begins to soften around the edges. This heart practice is supported by compassion and holds the wide view of equanimity:

If a child lives with criticism,
He learns to condemn;
If a child lives with hostility,
He learns to fight;
If a child lives with ridicule,
He learns to be shy;
If a child lives with jealousy,
He learns to feel guilty;
If a child lives with tolerance,
He learns to be patient;
If a child lives with encouragement,
He learns confidence;
If a child lives with praise,
He learns to appreciate;
If a child lives with fairness,

127

He learns justice;

If a child lives with security,

He learns to have faith;

If a child lives with approval,

He learns to like himself;

If a child lives with acceptance and friendship,

He learns to find love in the world.[13]

As educators, mental health professionals, activists, organizers, and all kinds of interrupters—we hold a unique positionality to create a new way of how we relate to each other. We can decide the culture we want to live within and can begin to unpack the normalized violence that we were taught in order to create communities of belonging and joy. This capacity and need to belong is rooted in our nature. So, too, is our ability to hold both joy and sorrow together, all at once.

Equanimity

Upekkha: Near enemy—indifference; far enemy—anxiety, greed

When something was important, the Buddha made sure it was repeated over and over again throughout the teachings. To make sure these teachings were carried as an oral tradition for anywhere from one hundred to five hundred years after his death, the Buddha made sure they were remembered through chants, parables, and lists.

Lots and lots of lists!

Equanimity was incredibly important to the Buddha in that it makes an appearance in the four heart practices of the Brahmaviharas, the Seven Factors of Awakening, and in the Ten *Paramis*, these perfections of heart and mind.

I have tried to receive this important lesson well, but it is challenging. An early instruction from a teacher that I hold dear was to allow the Dharma to wash over me . . . to know that what is meant to be known will eventually reveal itself.

And that is not possible in a body that is grasping or leaning in head first. This wisdom emerges from a body that is rested and receptive.

And that's really hard because we live in a culture that asks us to respond to every single emotion by either clicking a button or taking this pill; we've been so conditioned to *manage* all that arises—and equanimity is inviting us into stillness: *tatra-majjhattatā*—to stand in the middle.

Thích Nhất Hạnh sums it up by saying, "Life is both dreadful and wonderful. To practice meditation is to be in touch with both aspects."[14]

So, how do we stay in touch with the ten thousand joys and the ten thousand sorrows?[15]

I've always loved Pablo Neruda's poem "Keeping Quiet," an imagining of what it would be like to have a life that just stopped for a moment: no war, no violence, no rush . . . a life that allowed for a great hush to fall over the world. Time without interruption or a to-do list, time to just be. Neruda says: "let's stop for one second, / and not move our arms so much."[16]

These words really resonate with me. As a person who had historically been more of a doer and who considered the impact later, it never occurred to me that I could stop for one second and not move my arms so much; it was a revelation, and an invitation to understand myself in relation to my practice and how I moved through the world. To understand the origins of wisdom, the ongoing practice of liberation and joy.

Over these last few years, I've been tentative about moving my arms. Not because of uncertainty or doubt, but because there simply needed to be stillness in my body. And from that stillness and that quietness, I've been able to become aware of the violence within me, the rage, the anger, the fear. And this isn't alarming or scary; rather, I have a felt sense of the fullness of my humanity coming online. I can feel both the tension and the spaciousness in my body, the complexity of it all. And I needed the absence of sound and to engage with a different kind of movement of body to touch into it.

And so, as I am aware of this violence that I am born of, I am also aware of my capacity to be with it, to not let it take over, to see what is wanting to be witnessed.

Equanimity is a practice of a fierce heart. It allows us to go directly into the fire to see what's present, what needs to be tended to. Equanimity is not afraid, it does not back down, it stays present to whatever is arising. It allows us to be expansive in a very narrow and tight place.

I often think of equanimity as love + tenderness + clear boundaries, without attachment to the outcome. And this is where a lot of us get caught up. When we hear the word *boundaries*, we think of cruelty, of kicking someone out.

We tend to conflate equanimity with apathy or not caring, its near enemy.

What it means, though, is that if I want peace and ease in my life, and you bring chaos, I have to create this boundary because I care about you, and I can't have you hurting me.

It means that I can walk you to the front door of an AA meeting, but I can't go in and find recovery for you.

As one of my old bosses said when we ran a community center, "I'm not kicking you out of my heart, but I'm kicking you out of the space today."

It's an act of violence to demand someone be what we want them to be, to expect that they're going to respond in the same way that we would. And, so, equanimity can show up as an act of love as we give folks space to simply be themselves.

Classic Buddhist teachings describe this as all Beings are the owners of their karma; their happiness and unhappiness depend upon their actions, not on my wishes for them. It says that I care about you, and I'm not in control of the unfolding of events. I can't make it all better for you—which can feel incredibly difficult or incredibly liberating.

Equanimity helps us to know what belongs to you, and what belongs to me, and what belongs to our ancestors, as we often carry their burdens on top of ours.

Many of us are conditioned, even formally trained, to hold the hearts and suffering of others . . . which are simply not ours to hold. We can walk alongside, but we don't have to carry all of the baggage.

So when Neruda says, "let's stop for one second, / and not move our arms so much," he is giving us the opportunity to stand in the middle, to cultivate stillness, so that we're not running away from or pushing away, so that we can have an intimate knowing of what needs to be tended to and be able to witness what is arising, no matter how painful or scary.[17]

The Undefended Heart

These practices are not something to be believed in or not; to "believe" in something, the mind gets locked into a theory and uses useful energy to defend what it is we believe in. When we embody the heart practices of the Brahmaviharas, these divine abodes, that energy is turned toward nourishing an undefended heart. An undefended heart is rooted in courage and does not turn away when it is faced with injustice and violence. It allows the felt sense of anger and rage to be known and decides to use it as a catalyst toward skillful action and change. It allows us, unapologetically, to center compassion, loving kindness, joy, and equanimity in a world that is broken and bruised, and to turn toward it—knowing that we are protected.

LIBERATORY
FUTURES

7

BREATH. FUGITIVITY. WILD HORSES

Black, Ecocritical Feminist Strategies for Healing in a Predatory Empire

Valorie Thomas

I am broken. Little pieces of me lay along a stone path in a dark winter wood and I am afraid to run back for them.

—TRASI JOHNSON, "A Spell of Finding"

If we think of urban life as a location where black folks learned to accept a mind/body split that made it possible to abuse the body, we can better understand the growth of nihilism and despair in the black psyche. And we can know that when we talk about healing that psyche we must also speak about restoring our connection to the natural world.

—BELL HOOKS, *Sisters of the Yam*

Black breath is targeted, as we well know, but we should also recognize the potential of breathwork as a decolonizing modality in a time of suffocation, silencing, hyperpolicing, social implosion, lack of accountability, freefall. I think of breath practice as particularly relevant to our new Covidian vertigo and its ever-shifting disorientations, injustices, morbidity, and violent distortions because breathwork is one tool of replenishment in this time of global fatigue and indeterminacy brought on by seemingly insurmountable forces of oppression, destabilization, and death. Breath to cultivate agency is a bridge to the healing radiance that can still be witnessed in this turbulent world, and I protect that claim *fiercely*. At the same time, and this is a lesson about recognizing the inherent nonbinaries of vertiginous conditions, I refuse to willingly merge with the anxiety of oppressive systems while continuing to advocate for decolonizing, healing, and reimagining freedom.

If there is something I would offer to anyone seeking to act on behalf of their own healing without benefit of external resources, it is practicing vagus nerve activation by breathing in to a count of four and breathing out to a count of six or more. This simple technique does not require formal meditation but has the capacity anywhere, anytime, to regulate the nervous system by way of breathing; it is an antidote to the fight/flight/freeze/appease response of a triggered sympathetic nervous system, to adrenal overload and fatigue, to overproduction of cortisol, and it balances the amygdala and hippocampus.[1] I think of vagus breathing as a means of decolonizing our nervous systems through self-regulation of the trauma response, releasing stress, and activating the body's triune (heart-brain-gut) coherence, laying a foundation for anchoring from within that can impact how we stay present and grounded in the moment, respond to unpredictable circumstances, and hold agency by first establishing sovereignty of our own breath.

In my view, meditation, breathwork, and my connection to horses are personal necessities for surviving and healing in this time of predatory neoliberal empire. I encourage those of us engaging in social justice activism to craft similar restorative and relational practices that resonate with our beloved passions, to any degree possible and with any available resources, even if the resource is simply your own breath, which, at times, is all I've had available.

I have been a Bhakti yogi and meditator for thirty years and have been fascinated by horses in the abstract and in the flesh my whole life. The horse is my archetype of inspiration and survivorship. Though I haven't always been able to afford to have a horse, now I find increasing opportunities to interact with horses through volunteering at horse rescue organizations, veterans organizations, equine-supported therapy programs, and Equine Facilitated Learning programs.

Before horses came into my adult life, I had talismans, artwork, and ceramics of horses, as well as boots meant for riding, and I cultivated my dreams and knowledge of horses as healers. Sometimes being there for ourselves means conjuring to the manifestation of ourselves as possibility against all odds and other people's projections.

Wealth was a serious barrier; horses come with high costs. In grad school I taught, tutored, cleaned houses, and sold clothes when I needed money to pay rent and put food on the table. Later, as a professor, I managed to have an income that could support taking care of two rescued horses on a modest scale, allowing me just enough room to make the choice that would—among all possible options I was able to feel—best allow me to breathe.

I come from working-class roots, started working at the age of twelve, worked all through college and graduate school, and was a single parent throughout graduate school and my early career. I am a survivor of sexual trauma, domestic violence, and racial assault. I did not always have community or safe space. I was ambushed by predatory student loans and unethical lawyers, many of my early colleagues engaged in lateral violence under the blind eye of uninformed, dismissive administrators, and many of my colleagues normalized ableism and indulged in professionally undermining discriminatory tactics. Many times, my survival resources literally came down to a small circle of trusted family, extended family, my body, and my practices, including meditation and breathwork.

Developing restorative practices that carried reminders of grace became pivotal to surviving grad school at UC Berkeley as a Black working-class single parent; to completing my scholarly work and activism as a Black woman working-class professor in an all-white English department at a predominantly white institution; to managing my neurodivergence in a neurotypical dominant profession; and later, to contending with Covid and its aftermath. I would learn to find healing in the community—especially through experiencing the arts, film, and music; through service; and through being outdoors, building a network of healing practitioners, and attaining spiritual engagement—guided by my determination to be alive with well-being to the fullest extent possible. This orientation sustained me through Long Covid, financial stress, anti-Black professional conflict, a late AuDHD diagnosis, and the loss of friends and loved ones among the many dead and dying worldwide due to the pandemic and imploding social conditions.

As an interdisciplinary scholar in African American literature, African Diaspora studies, and Afrofuturism/Black Speculative studies, I ask my students to reconsider their relationship to embodiment on their own terms, their relationship to community, and their relationship to place. We study networks of relationship beyond the human and beyond dominance over nature. With this work, we begin to decolonize, reindigenize, and reorient from their sense of how it is to be them, pushing back against ideas of the individual as an alienated intellect isolated from and at war with the body, nature, and cosmos. I encourage students to investigate the experience of meditative breath as a modality that may support understanding of voice, sonic/rhythmic/vibrational presence, liberatory aspirations, and *ontoepistemological wherewithal*—the how, why, when, and where logics of diasporic consciousness and literacies.[2] We discuss what it can mean to move beyond thinking abstractly about centering African diaspora knowledge by acting to welcome, rather than dismiss, Black liberatory thought in spaces where the default system exalts the norms of white settler colonialism. What if we apply African diasporic critical thought as embodied practice in organizations? What would happen, for instance, if we really identify and dismantle misogynoir in organizations?[3]

What if we practice centering the thought and lives of Black women, not as an abstract concept, but operating and setting policy from the guidance of the Combahee River Collective Statement, that "If Black women were free, it would mean that everyone else would have to be free since our freedom would necessitate the destruction of all the systems of oppression"?[4]

These are the kinds of Black speculative and Black feminist questions that I use to frame my institutional role and my fight for access to resources to create scholarly work, teaching practices, and community-centered programming that center Blackness, Indigeneity, and decolonizing thought whenever possible. But this Black speculative opposition to embedded white supremacist norms and predatory agendas can apply to any institution or organization struggling with what it means to move from diversity as a quantified data point to a continuum of antiracism-intersectionality-equity as a daily process. This stance became the starting point for organizing symposia and community- and practitioner-centered programming such as *Healing Ways: Decolonizing Our Minds, Our Bodies, Ourselves*; for organizing symposia and programming on Afrofuturisms; and for curating the 2015 art exhibition, programming, and symposium *Vertigo@Midnight: New Visual AfroFuturisms & Speculative Migrations* as offshoots of my interdisciplinary pedagogy in multiple literature-based courses.[5] In 1998, as the first African American, or BIPOC of any persuasion, professor of English at the elite liberal arts college where I was hired out of grad school, I chose to teach strategically in this setting in ways that centered decolonizing; Black feminist/womanist theory; Indigeneity; and BIPOC, queer, and otherwise marginalized students' experiences in dialogue with my interdisciplinary research and pedagogy.[6]

In teaching, I prioritize social justice, equity, decolonizing, and encouraging all students to investigate literature and the arts in complex relationship to their particular lives. We see race. I teach as a Black feminist, but I also enter every class with an open syllabus; if students want to approach the topics and reading through the lens of their own backgrounds, histories, cultural orientations, and bodies, so be it. I am a proponent of somatic work, inclusivity, and healing-centered engagement—sometimes reclaiming information and wisdom traditions across millennia—in order to reconfigure connections to collective sensibilities, intuitive practices, bodies, lives, places, and futures. (Be prepared for cynics and those who are threatened by unfamiliar Indigenous, decolonial, and non-Western modalities to casually dismiss these practices as, for example, "woo woo," or to be otherwise contemptuous or hostile—nonetheless, we continue doing the work, and sometimes it is about reconnecting with ancestors and grappling with why it was that colonizers sought to obliterate and demonize the spiritual knowledge of the colonized, and how to bring those traditions back to our intellectual lives and critical awareness.) In my classrooms, while acknowledging that the trauma in the books and artwork we study mirrors the trauma in our lives, families, and communities, it is not enough, and it is not ethical enough, to focus only on trauma in a circular and compartmentalized way that leaves us retraumatized. We move through it by releasing and rebalancing through movement, voice, play, celebration, song, laughter, reconnection, affirmation, and reflection, and through offering support, nourishment (literal and figurative), joy, grounding, gratitude, and compassionate self-acceptance.

Black feminist theory and womanism hold the center of any course I teach. If we examine the impact of the slave trade on a novel or film, for instance, we also consider a continuum that contests the assumption that these systems are past/over by framing current debt and carceral structures as neoliberal Middle Passage/enslavement/sharecropping, insofar as these structures enforce predatory tactics in Black communities and continue to disrupt families, criminalize communities, and dehumanize Black bodies. We acknowledge and deepen our understanding of the impact and trauma of genocide, enslavement, invasion, land theft, policed borders, erasure, forced amnesia, and lives dominated by compulsory labor. It is intentional that we then work toward reintegrating ourselves in community and continuing toward liberatory goals. While reclaiming memories and histories of epigenetic and generational trauma, grief, and longing, we might, for example, look to emergent strategy and gather to celebrate survivorship, honor our individual and shared stories, and imagine and claim our futurities.[7] In my classes, we build community by gathering not only to analyze texts in class discussion, but also to collaborate as we share time, stories, and activities related to our experiences and draw connections to the subjects we study. We may cook, eat, meditate, dance, sing, chant, or make art and poetry. We use the classroom as a place to practice holding space for trust in self and others. This is intended to be a pedagogy of trying new ways of imagining. As I learned from my students year by year, this sharing evolved from spontaneous improvisational moments to become an intentional final gathering at the end of the class that features art and performance by students as well as scholarship they may choose to share. It is an exercise in holding space and practicing acceptance, in which students have space to define whatever the semester has meant to them or reflect on the time and their process.

Along the way in my teaching, one by one, too many BIPOC, queer, first gen, working-class, marginalized students either started showing up in my office broken, or sometimes they literally or figuratively disappeared. I'd learn of emotional suffering, illness, and academic crises *after* the fact. It happened too frequently to be thought of as isolated incidents. They were keeping up a game face until they weren't; dogged by impostor syndrome; often feeling out of place and out of control. Racial stress was a frequent theme regardless of the students' particular background. They came to my office, usually struggling to project a "professional" demeanor, sometimes tearing up, hyperventilating, unable to catch their breath. Why were so many brilliant, highly motivated students navigating the same isolation, and what institutional support could be assembled to mitigate the stress before it reached the crisis point? I have criticisms of the all-encompassing culture of professionalism, or as Leah Goodridge comments in "Professionalism as a Racial Construct," upon consideration, "I began to see that professionalism itself was a mechanism to put people of color in place in the workplace."[8] We should not, in my opinion, be teaching students to be slaves to professionalism at the expense of their emotional well-being, cultural complexity, and humanity. Analyzing how concepts of professionalism in organizations have been aligned with racism, researchers specify how characteristics of white supremacy translate to the idea of professional conduct in the workplace.[9] Professionalism has not been as neutral as it seems; in fact, it has encoded bias and needs to be uncoupled from racism and racist structures through critical analysis.

A prominent characteristic of white supremacy in organizations is recognizable when "making a mistake is confused with being a mistake, doing wrong with being wrong."[10] This unexamined organizational culture—especially when anti-Blackness and anti-Indigeneity frontload the presumption that BIPOC individuals are beholden, suspect, mistaken, and incompetent—suffocates diversity, keeps organizations out of touch, and harms people. Noting that the impact of white supremacy culture is complex and elusive, and thus should be clearly identified, Tema Okun argues:

> Culture is powerful precisely because it is so present and at the same time so very difficult to name or identify. The characteristics [of white supremacy] are damaging because they are used as norms and standards without being proactively named or chosen by the group. They are damaging because they promote white supremacy thinking. Because we all live in a white supremacy culture, these characteristics show up in the attitudes and behaviors of all of us—people of color and white people. Therefore, these attitudes and behaviors can show up in any group or organization, whether it is white-led or predominantly white or people of color–led or predominantly people of color.[11]

This socialization begins in educational systems that normalize white upper-class values while stigmatizing and policing decolonial and BIPOC knowledge as, at best, quaint but unserious niche concerns, and immaterial to the broader and more sophisticated economy of ideas, ambitions, and achievements. What is comfortable for the colonizer, however, has zero bearing on the well-being of marginalized subjects' thinking in resistance to colonialism and acting freely in educational settings.

Many of us can attest to the "invisibility of Black women as the unvoiced, unseen everything that is not white."[12] We contend with this racial invisibility yet are hyperscrutinized. Many Black women students who made their way to my office shared confidential testimonies consistent with what Paula Miley terms "emotional and physical responses permeating all aspects of life consistent with Complex Racial Trauma (CoRT)."[13] Students tended to feel there were no safe avenues for reporting their experiences of racial trauma due to the risk of being labeled difficult, dramatic, a problem, or a whiner. This situation might register as an institutional crisis if your organization values antiracism. According to the research,

> *Similar to complex trauma, racial trauma surrounds the victims' life course and engenders consequences on their physical and mental health, behavior, cognition, relationships with others, self-concept, and social and economic life . . . One of the important aspects of racial trauma is its ubiquity and omnipresence in the life of racialized people . . . In addition to the pervasiveness and consistency of racial discrimination and trauma in racialized people's personal lives at systemic and institutional levels, they occur in their neighborhoods, schools, workplace, social and health services, and economic and financial services on a repetitive, multiple, and cumulative basis.*[14]

And similarly:

> *Racial trauma, a form of race-based stress, refers to People of Color and Indigenous individuals' (POCI) reactions to dangerous events and real or perceived experiences of racial discrimination. Such experiences may include threats of harm and injury, humiliating and shaming events, and witnessing racial discrimination toward other POCI. Although*

similar to posttraumatic stress disorder, racial trauma is unique in that
it involves ongoing individual and collective injuries due to exposure
and reexposure to race-based stress.[15]

Given this data, implying that the reality ceases to apply because
people enter an organizational bubble is, at best, disingenuous. Black
women frequently attest to being silenced, ignored, outrageously micro-
aggressed, and socially conflicted in the fishbowl of contemporary US
institutional life in ways that reflect Hortense Spillers's observation that
Black women are "reified into a status of non-being."[16] In the context of
education, I wonder about the impact of such experiences on Black wom-
en's efforts to excel as students, as faculty, as leaders, and in our overall
well-being. Is there equity in learning when, in a triggered sympathetic
nervous system's response to trauma/danger/attack, the human brain
is incapable of absorbing and processing information while in survival
(fight/flight/freeze/appease) mode, while privileged others have consistently protected psychological safety? What is it to be a Black woman
student at a predominantly white institution who must confront questions
about whether or not dominant systems are relegating her, in unstated
but nonetheless forceful terms, to non-being in a historical loop in which
Black women continue to be treated this way? Black women have historically been positioned by white supremacy as "the principal point of passage between the human and the non-human world . . . In other words,
the Black person mirrored for the society around her what a human was
not."[17] Non-persons. Having been an African American woman student,
I can say that Black women, and all BIPOC students, deserve better in
education.[18] I've definitely been called a complainer on these issues, and
I have been described as everything from "loud and inappropriate" to
"mean," "angry," "overbearing," "a bitch," "a bully," and "a diva," and this
too is gendered, raced, and classed policing. As Sara Ahmed theorizes,

To be heard as complaining is not to be heard. To hear someone as
complaining is an effective way of dismissing someone. You do not have

144

to listen to the content of what she is saying if she is just complaining or always complaining . . . Racism is often enacted by the dismissal of racism as complaint.[19]

BIPOC students in perceived or actual oppositional tension to colonial systems are at a disadvantage due to power differentials in universities. They risk retribution from faculty, administrators, and even peers who wield grades, approval, rewards, and the promise of inclusion, thus gatekeeping futures by keeping dissenters/complainers in line under threat of negative evaluations and exclusion. From all indications, I was witnessing students in distress from being socialized to *uncritically* uphold what has been called "the bias threshold," but no one with institutional influence questioned whether this socialization was happening, or how it might align with unspoken settler colonial imperatives:

One of the primary ways it shows up is in the expectation for people of color to have to endure abusive, toxic, racist behavior. And by doing so, the prize is to be perceived as the utmost consummate professional . . . this ideology that you have to have a thick skin and also that you're prized for having a thick skin and for putting up with . . . the reasonable person is literally supposed to be someone who is raceless, genderless, no culture . . . it ascribes to a white normative . . . we are taught to strip away emotions.[20]

Emotions related to the desire to have felt safety and belonging, to have intellectual inclusion, and to have appropriate access to resources don't cease because they're ignored. BIPOC students encountering these issues were routinely coming to my door expecting to be shamed. They had been admitted to a highly selective college and thereby were positioned as high achieving, special, and successful—they were also, in all cases I recall, genuinely capable, dedicated, and well meaning, and they were striving, not only for themselves, but to not let down anyone they cared about. Years of striving had taught them to make excellence look effortless. They had absorbed the idea that professionalism is about never being needy, vulnerable, or a burden. Needing anything, especially help, could be read as weakness, or worse, incompetence.

I'm not a clinician and don't offer diagnoses or medical advice. I made it a practice to mostly listen, taking care not to be judgmental, to suggest strategies for navigating their academic work where possible, to refer many to Student Affairs and to the student health and counseling centers (if they wanted that support), and if they wanted to find outside referrals, I encouraged them to do so. I understand the wish not to be exposed, possibly stigmatized, or to become the focus of gossip on a small campus, especially if there are so few BIPOC students that they stand out all the time anyway and are aware of the tension of being both hypervisible and invisible at the same time.

When the pattern of racial trauma became visible, I began to wonder what students' experiences have to tell us about the status of inclusion in this moment. I came to realize that many BIPOC, first generation, working-class, disabled, and otherwise marginalized students had been socialized to internalize systemic failures and conflicts not as structural violence but as incompetence and personal failure.[21] They blamed themselves even when they could sense or identify systemic conflicts. A student/individual should never be saddled with the task of either excusing or trying to correct organizational failures on their own. This situation, particularly as it affected a disproportionate number of Black women, prompted me to brainstorm interventions; the most logical path seemed to be starting a conversation around literature, art, and personal narrative at the intersection of health/healing, race, history, language, and cultural knowledge. It seemed useful to bring the language and stories of well-being to the classroom; to cultivate a space in which to scrutinize how we narrate the "human" and the "healthy," the "cured" and "disabled" body as organized under colonial racial and gender regimes; and to explore alternatives. What might it look like to experiment with building or finding strategic counternarratives while expanding literacy around the medical-industrial

complex as a feature of colonial empire? In particular, we might welcome the stories in which we reject being silenced, reprimanded, and
pathologized.

bell hooks writes of similar dynamics in *Sisters of the Yam*:

*When black female students would come to my office after reading these
novels and confess the truth of their lives . . . I was shocked . . . Our
collective hope for the group was that it would be a space where black
women could name their pain and find ways of healing . . . choosing
"wellness" as an act of political resistance . . . It is important that black
people talk to one another, that we talk with friends and allies, for the
telling of our stories enables us to name our pain, our suffering, and to
seek healing . . . Healing occurs through testimony, through gathering
together everything available to you and reconciling.[22]*

I don't propose to "heal" anyone and wouldn't promise to do so in
a class, even implicitly; in fact, my students taught me that no one is
obligated to heal, anyhow. I could, however, design a class grounded in
a Black feminist speculative ethos that would be a space for examining
displacement and racial trauma, that would welcome stories and critical
reflections, a space for building community. The class would assemble an
archive of materials to further conversation. This was an opportunity to
concretize and give material form to invisible, hard-to-put-into-words,
elusive or unseen, unacknowledged, maybe unmentionable experience;
a Black speculative space in which students would affirm their particular
truths and stories in a non-judgmental, non-shaming, collective space in
which we would strive to be only witnesses and supporters of people piec-
ing together their experiences, thoughts, meanings, and needs. I aimed to
contemplate testimonies of being out of place and body—fugitive stories—
through generating contrary formations of Black womanist speculative
space in the classroom.

If we set an intention to practice putting shame and being judgmental
aside, could we short-circuit this ingrained mechanism? Would students

147

want to tell their stories as counternarratives, reimaginings, empowering insurgencies, social critiques, and parts of larger historical continuums? I hoped the classroom could be a space for sitting with questions about how language, intersectionality, and dominant social scripts impact their health and for investigating what healing means to them and their communities by understanding structural violence and racialized freedom as foundational to shaping what we mean by health/healing. As undergraduates, my friends and I encountered identical racialized conflicts and shame, the same pressure to produce and achieve while burying emotions and stories relevant to our daily well-being and health. How could these young thinkers be encountering the same institutional silences? In response, I developed a course titled Healing Narratives in the spirit of one of my mentors, Professor VèVè Amasasa Clark, by using the classroom as a communal space where students could both engage critical analysis of the topic of health and healing and contemplate their lives, histories, cultural complexity, beliefs, and emotions in the context of taking control of their own stories of suffering and wellness.

I thought an English class could put the question of BIPOC and marginalized people's health on the table through fiction, memoir, poetry, performance, music, and visual arts, as well as in creative nonfiction and critical work. We could practice radical self-acceptance; probe historical and social events, public policy, and ideology; and interrogate race, gender, and class in connection with theories of the human, illness, and disability. This would include studying settler colonialism and the colonized, enslaved body; and confronting genocide, land theft, structural violence, how suffering is understood, and how racial and social disparities inform the medical system. We would also start building/reclaiming literacies in decolonial and Indigenous approaches to medicine, health, and healing. Maybe students would find a space in which to take stock of the unannounced tolls and taxes that racism and systemic violence enact on bodies and communities. Maybe they would feel encouraged to reclaim self-love as radical social justice practice and take a pause on capitalism's nonstop grind culture.[23] Maybe it would be a space in which they could think together about mutual aid and what healing-centered engagement might look like, rather than absorbing a steady diet of trauma.

Students who were drawn to take this course would have the experience of feeling welcome *as is* and of being enough, and we would breathe into this recognition as a community. At a minimum, they would walk away knowing that complex racial trauma exists and develop an idea of contexts and a working familiarity with relevant histories. Students would learn that Black people in the time of slavery were judged non-sentient and unable to feel pain; that "Drapetomania" was a clinical diagnosis applied by doctors and slaveowners to explain the purported "illness" that caused slaves to run away; that Sarah Baartman, of the Khoi-Khoi in South Africa, was taken to Paris in 1814 to be displayed as a scientific specimen and entertainment attraction known as The Venus Hottentot. Onstage and in private viewings, Baartman's body and genitalia were presented to white audiences and medical scholars as clinical proof that Black bodies were the antithesis of the human, the normal, and the civilized. Baartman died at age twenty-six and then anthropologists dissected her, placing her genitals, brain, and skeleton on public display in the Musée de l'Homme until 1985. This kind of information would expand students' comprehension of the evolution of Western medicine as it intersects with race, gender, sexuality, class, disability, mortality, and the concept of the human. We would discuss forced sterilization, biopolitics, scientific racism, the covert harvesting of Henrietta Lacks's cells to develop the HeLa cell line, the Tuskegee syphilis experiment, reproductive justice and genocide, and how human zoos served empire and eugenics. We would read *Beloved* with the understanding that enslaved Black women were reduced to animal status and body parts: assemblages of hands, arms, genitals, backs, legs, wombs. We would study the evolution of medical apartheid in the West.[24] The students who inspired the course lived the liminal experience of feeling on the run in spaces that were expected to be welcoming; we needed to discuss readings about fugitivity, interstitiality, and the speculative as a call to form alternative/underground/rebel community and counternarratives that drew on lived experience to resist colonialist gaslighting.[25]

The Healing Narratives course led to organizing a week-long public symposium and programming called *Healing Ways: Decolonizing Our Minds, Our Bodies, Ourselves.* The title is a mashup of Ngũgĩ wa Thiong'o's *Decolonizing the Mind* and the groundbreaking feminist health handbook, *Our Bodies, Ourselve*s.[26] *Healing Ways* came about because students felt strongly about expanding their conversations from Healing Narratives beyond the classroom and putting into practice an inclusive, public facing, decolonial framework that would foreground the stories, cultures, and experiences of multiple communities. There was helpful interest from colleagues, some administrators, students, and alumni. Health justice activists and healing practitioners agreed to provide information, educate about ancestral knowledge traditions, lead workshops, guide rituals, and share empowering modalities. Practitioners were paid or chose to donate their time; events were free, open to the public, and welcoming to children and adults. We were not defining health, what healing is, or promising cures; we were attempting to open a space that affirms dialogue and promotes the development of inclusive, interdisciplinary healing literacies that lead to empowerment and choice. We wanted to treat the time as a lab to experiment with decolonizing the academic environment with students at the center, presenting workshops, organizing, and proactively utilizing institutional resources on behalf of communities (especially less-resourced communities) beyond the borders of campus. I aimed to draw the broadest possible community of healers, bodyworkers, somatic practitioners, scholars, artists, writers, musicians, dancers, yogis, elders, spiritual workers, filmmakers, poets, and activists to campus—anyone interested in healing and social justice.[27] In turn, participants were invited to structure programming and invite other participants. We relied on word of mouth and social media to get the word out. The programming particularly amplified the voices oriented toward decolonizing, intersectional praxis, and Indigenous, diasporic, and non-Western knowledge traditions.[28]

We expanded the schedule throughout the week, working to accom-modate as many presenters and participants as wanted to be a part of the program. Students created pop-up events including art exhibitions, open mic spoken word performances, writing workshops, meditation sessions, music, dance, and mobile libraries. Cambodian American poet Kosal Khiev Skyped in for a live reading from Cambodia—having sent us his clothing to place in a chair as an installation marking the fact of his deportation from the US. We also collaborated with the campus organic farm to install a public labyrinth built from local river rocks. One student told the campus newspaper in an interview:

> *Healing is something I've denied myself too many times before, dealing with guilt over how I feel and what I'm struggling through—and this is something I've seen in my friends and family as well. When I heard that Healing Ways was actually going to happen, I immediately jumped on board. It seemed like an awesome opportunity for definitions of and tools for healing to become part of the dialogue on campus . . . For as long as I can remember, writing has been critical in navigating my iden-tity and emotional terrain, in facing what it is that's bothering me and take steps toward addressing it, and that's something I'd like to share. I don't have a good sense of how the campus has reacted to Healing Ways, but I hope participants walk away with the motivation to incorporate methods of healing into their own lives.*[29]

Another student offered:

> *Environmental stuff and Healing Ways are very closely related. Through a greater awareness of how environments are structured and shaped—and by environment, I mean physical and figurative spaces—whether in a national park, in a housing unit in the middle of an urban center, or in the QRCs [Queer Resource Centers] figurative space, we come to a better understanding of how processes of hurting and healing might exist there . . . The labyrinth is part of the [campus] farm's goals to*

become a more multipurpose space where healing and reconnection to land are key. Basically, the farm is trying to bridge the gap that exists too often in mainstream environmentalism, and even in the farm's past, between environmental health and human needs or justice.[30]

Healing Ways opened an immersive, culturally complex space in real-time that modeled equity, intersectionality, and mutual support. The labyrinth we built at the farm as a usable art installation represented the week's overarching ethos of making a space of sanctuary attuned to transformation, mobility, and insight. Many reflected on the power of remembrance, on bringing diverse streams of fugitive knowledge into confluence, and on the replenishing impact of art, sharing stories, and bearing witness. Each activity held an invitation to divest ourselves of judgmental reactions rooted in colonial, racialized, ableist, anti-Black, anti-Indigenous, heteronormative dominance. Over a few days, we made time for critical inquiry informed by an array of cultural and political orientations while participants found opportunities to put decolonial intentions and care into action. It was an access point for strengthening agency through reclaiming ancestral and Indigenous knowledge and practices, asserting body sovereignty and self-determination, depathologizing and demystifying our experiences, and resisting isolation. This was time and space devoted to theorizing fugitivity and freedom, gathering counternarratives that refute the prerogatives of predatory empire, affirming survivance, and disrupting colonial assumptions about who we are, what we think and do, how we should be, and how we imagine the future.

At the heart of these various snapshots is the fact that these strategies can be adapted to any group and are meant to be improvisational, imaginative, and open to experimentation around the question of how we pool our knowledge and skills to create space, even temporarily, that reflects an ethos of "if we decolonize in this or any moment, what does that look like, feel like, sound, smell, and taste like, and what are we pouring into reimagining ourselves, each other, and our experience?" It can

start by us simply refusing the widely accepted habit of being annihilat-
ingly judgmental and punitive in ways that perpetuate structural violence
such as racial and cultural gatekeeping, diminishing others, hoarding
resources, mobbing, and scapegoating. Any organization can deepen the
practice of authentic inclusion as an antidote to hypervigilant colonialist
gatekeeping. We can do the opposite of what systems of colonial domination demand by taking the space and time to notice what we notice
and respect what we notice. We suffer from structural violence and are
depleted by monocultural colonial social systems and racial capitalism,
but we can deploy available institutional resources to share knowledge of
not only resistance but the necessity—especially for activists and cultural
workers—to replenish, heal, and be comforted.

I learned along with my students to practice well-being by reclaiming
what I love on a daily basis. I feel joy in connection with horses. Many
people are unable to fathom my affinity for horses; people have com-
mented that Black people don't connect with nature. Does it have to be
said these are harmful stereotypes? Nature and recreation, including the
horse world, are as colonized as the rest of US society. BIPOC struggles
include taking #LandBack, decolonizing settler geographies, establishing fugitive space, and reimagining relationships with places and fellow
beings. My education with horses has included learning to take care of
them with compassion and as my honored relations since early childhood.
This relationship restores my spirit, relieves stress, and balances energy,
and it is one way I express speculative fugitivity, through Black feminist,
Afrofuturist, decolonial, self-reclamation. If you see me with a horse, I am
claiming my joy and receiving their teachings, and trying to make their
lives better. On a larger level, BIPOC and marginalized horse people shat-
ter the settler myth of an all-white West. I track my imaginative lineage
back to horse cultures in Africa dating to 1600 BCE.[31] As an urban Black
woman activist-scholar of Indigenous Mamaceqtaw/Menominee ances-
try, I am grounded in the integrity of my relationship with horses, the
willing adjustments I make to secure this way of life, the flows of nature

they guide me into, and honoring Afro-Indigenous ancestral spiritual knowledge.

In 2009, after over twenty years of missing horses in my life while focusing on academia, I decided to listen to my well-being, which was saying that I should go back and pick up this sovereign piece of myself; this piece that aligns my sense of being, a flowing river of *Ashé* (Yoruba: "life force"), source, balance, spiritual coherence. Nobody else had to understand it or approve of it. I understood it. My Indigenous ancestors called this *horse medicine*. I acknowledged that my work necessitates continually recuperating and healing from structural violence and anti-Blackness, that academia with its roots firmly planted in anti-Blackness and settler-colonialism has never been safe or sufficient—and so, new non-negotiable: I would have horses in my life. I would lean into this meditation and never again allow what sustains my spiritual sovereignty to be pushed into the isolated distance. This was an act of self-retrieval.

I soon became guardian to two rescued mustangs, wild horses whose way of being in the world fills me with gratitude and neutralizes the many ways in which misogynoir, ableism, and white eugenicist capitalism continually deploy predatory tactics toward my being. Their status as herd animals who, contrary to popular myth, are largely regarded as vermin and hunted as pet food, meat export, and fertilizer, is not lost on me. It was not a given that these two discarded souls would survive. Working with horses and helping them recover from trauma teach me a new sense of balance that is continually adjusting. Everything I do comes from a spiritual connection to my ancestors flowing through the gift of horse medicine. They radiate healing.

Horses frequently offer a healing relationship to humans that invites us to consider ethics and how to be less extractive and objectifying. They do this by sensing us as we are—they can smell our emotional state; their hearts automatically coregulate and communicate with the herd in a larger electromagnetic field than ours, one that takes us in and supports regulating our nervous systems; they calm and balance our heart rates, blood pressure, brain waves, and neurochemicals. They respond honestly to care and kindness when given the opportunity. They have historically partnered with humans despite being hunted, prey animals. They have an exceptional ability to support therapeutic healing, recovery, recuperating from trauma, PTSD, and developing social-emotional skills; they even aid literacy education. We are able to offer them care when we aren't imposing demands. Simply paying attention reveals that their breath communicates their emotional state. Tuning into their breathing can be the foundation of our self-regulation, connection, collaboration, heart-mind-gut coherence, authenticity, and stillness.

Horses deepen my awareness of living in precarity—economic, racial, and gendered; their lives are characterized by uncertainty, yet they remain adaptable, and this capacity holds lessons about emotional intelligence. African American trainer and author Nahshon Cook offers this: "My life with the horse as meditation has taught me to see change as energetic shifts in the body, and the body as emotional memory."[32] The insights of this epistemology of the human-horse meditative relationship suggest new constructions of agency, ontological improvisations, and new archetypes of possibility—what we can recall, we can reimagine and sing into a new story.

For me as a Black woman, speculative fugitivity is a lived concept. I locate myself in the liminal space of freedom between breath and wild horses surviving the enclosures of a predatory empire. We all have our own medicine—in my view, reclaiming it means making contact, as best we can, with the elements that inspire us to feel grace, belonging, and healing when we need it. We all hold the ability to breathe into our futures like wild horses.

8

HEALING THROUGH LOVING-AWARENESS-IN-ACTION

Sará King and Davion "Zi" Ziere

This chapter outlines the Mobius Liberatory Healing Methodological Approach, an emergent model for developing accountability in organizations interested in the role of healing and embodying well-being as a central aspect of their way of orienting collectively and contributing toward the realization of a more healed society. Mobius is a not-for-profit organization whose mission is to activate and support a tech ecosystem focused on healing and liberation, prioritizing Black, Brown, Indigenous, queer people, and others marginalized by the dominant tech sector.

The purpose of this case study is to intimately reveal some of the inner workings of Mobius, an organization undergoing a conscientious process of embodying decolonization and accountability through the healing processes of its core members. This case study is written from the perspective of the Black-identified members of the team specifically, as this racialized social location and embodied identity uniquely informs our perspective on both what constitutes healing processes and how we have responded to instances of harm/oppression within the organization by reifying our dedication to embodying loving-awareness-in-action and liberation for the benefit of the entire team.[1] *Loving-awareness-in-action* in this particular instance means practicing transparency about our internal process of healing as an act and extension of the embodiment of social justice—it is an extension of our belief that social justice and well-being are one and the same.[2] This reorients our understanding of justice as a state of being shaped by love and being aware of the need for the prioritization of the individual and collective body's healing within the field of our shared interdependence. While the word *love* may mean many things to different people, in this instance we refer to love as the enactment of skillful empathy, fierce compassion, forgiveness, radical friendship, patience, kindness, enthusiastic uplift, extending grace and trust to one another, and a commitment to practicing nonviolence and healing-as-accountability. This is love from the heart, not just the head, love felt and known in the body, not only thought or imagined.

We hope this account provides a reflective space in which other organizations facing similar questions or issues of racialized relational rupture can understand how these ruptures intersect in ways that stem from the pain of unhealed intergenerational trauma and under-addressed patterns of domination. We hope this offering may resonate with others facing racialized ruptures in their own purposeful nonprofit work and that this methodology contributes to documenting different variations of healing methods for embodying accountability that are now emerging in the nonprofit sector.

This is also a story about an instance of reparations and repair from two Black people's perspective. We recognize that very few stories of reparations exist in the narrative of what it means to be a Black person born in the US, which makes this story quite radical. In a sense, facets of our story are common, in terms of the prevalence of ruptures brought about by racialized trauma inside of organizations; in other ways, our story is a story of the experience of rare levels of social, economic, relational, and even spiritual support. Our story may invite these questions: Why are stories of reparations and healing like ours so rare? What prevents stories of healing-as-accountability like ours from being more common? Our response to questions like these from the perspective of our lived experience is part of why we think this is a compelling story to share. We believe it will help people to envision what their own processes of repair will look like if healing is prioritized, centered, and well resourced in their organizations. Our story might also help to explain or contextualize why some efforts of healing-as-accountability fail when those attempting to enact the healing processes are drastically under-resourced, which we would argue is a vestige of systemic oppression and historically institutionalized harm. We understand that what we experienced might not pertain to or be feasible/appropriate within every organizational context, or between people who come from myriad social, economic, or geographical locations who are navigating instances of harm. Nonetheless, we hope this story is received as inspirational and supportive to anyone looking to center loving-awareness, radical trust, embodiment, and healing at the foundation of how they are evolving organizationally. Perhaps philanthropic organizations that support the work of promoting global well-being might consider how developing funds for the implementation of healing-as-accountability might generate significant collective healing impact for our society and the world. Indeed, our capacity to heal from collective trauma at scale might depend on this kind of innovative action and liberatory thinking.

At Mobius, we seek to discover what healing and liberation mean in organizational contexts, individually and collectively, to identify how the artifacts, products, events, and engagements that emerge from a variety of organizations and institutions can contribute to collective liberation more broadly on a societal level. By attempting to create a liberatory context from which to do labor, we believe and uphold that the people involved in the emergent process of organizational development have to be actively engaged in and dedicated to healing themselves, thereby revealing and embodying a greater depth of their authentic selves as expressions of love. The following quote from Zenju Earthlyn Manuel is a direct example of what we mean when we speak of liberation in this context:

There are many possible meanings or experiences of spiritual liberation as it emerges from within. I experience it as freedom from projections of superiority and inferiority among sentient beings. To experience libera-tion in such a way is to experience authentic compassion, wisdom, love, and interrelationship. Authentic experiences of these qualities do not come with ideas that someone is better or worse than anyone else. Liber-ation comes from within the body when we clearly see, not only with our eyes but with our hearts, who and what has erroneously claimed power and domination over others in this life; it is when we clearly see the dominance of one over others as fear and hatred manifested in action. Liberation from within affects both personal bodies and the collective body of living beings; it has both personal and social dimensions.[3]

To help develop liberatory technology by liberatory technologists who come primarily from marginalized backgrounds, with the central intention of creating technology that best supports their communities, the Mobius team decided to intentionally embark on the journey of self-decolonization to be a safe space within which liberatory technolo-gists could thrive. To be more specific, the Mobius space underwent a shift from being a white-dominant space that, in practice, unconsciously centered the experiences of white-bodied staff and white supremacy culture to being a space that actively sought the healing benefit of being an interracial coalition of freedom-dreamers.[4]

Because of the initial lack of diversity in Mobius's population, the team recognized that systems of oppression and domination were being repli-cated by the fact that only white-bodied people were represented in the organizational space. From the authors' perspective, white-bodied team members awakened to this harmful dynamic as a result of their exposure to social justice spaces, thought, and practices that were developed by marginalized thought leaders and activists, as well as their relationship with white abolitionists. This catalyzed a desire to integrate people of color who had the expertise and lived experience navigating and creating just, equitable spaces into the preexisting, white-bodied team in order to begin an embodied decolonization process. Incorporating Black-identified team members in the Mobius space catalyzed a dramatic shift toward a space that attempted to radically center the lived experiences and embodied expressions of the liberation of Black people. This shift represented the potential that Mobius could become a living working space into which others from marginalized backgrounds might find a place of belonging and healing. Though organizations that center the power, authority, and autonomy of white-bodied people, and therefore foreground white supremacy culture as "the norm," have made many efforts to retrofit, very few have successfully become organizations that are safe and inclusive for marginalized peoples. To speak metaphorically, from our perspective, those who have been given the power to create a table, as well as to determine who gets seats at said table, will remain in a position of disproportionate power until those who have been historically disempowered are given equal opportunity to create a table (and seats) for themselves. This doesn't mean that retrofitting organizations to be more diverse is not a worthy effort. We are pointing out the unique challenges that retrofitting for diversity represents.

Mobius started the process of formulating a healing methodology with a deceptively simple question: What would be the metrics by which "success" could be measured or ascertained when embodied liberation and healing are foregrounded as a stated goal of an organization? The answers to this question, though they are not conclusive and are only representative of the lived experiences of the Black-identified team members that are being shared in this context, are foregrounded in this text to the best of our ability. Because this text deliberately elevates our lived experiences as our primary and very personal examples of *healing-as-progress*, this is a fundamentally phenomenological account centering the embodied knowing, subjectivity, and intersubjectivity of Black-identified people in the Mobius space as an example of what might be possible in other organizational spaces that are aligning themselves with the work of decolonization and *healing-as-liberation*. The processes of embodied liberation and decolonization, in our thinking, are possibly so intertwined as to be one and the same.

161

A Journey of Decolonization

Our journey as the Mobius Collective began with a shared desire to create Beloved Community across perceived lines of difference to support the development of *Liberatory Technology*, or technology that supports collective well-being, thriving, wholeness, and aliveness. Liberatory Technology is a term that emerged from the Mobius space, springing from our collective acknowledgment of the vast and systemic harms that have been and continue to be created by those who develop technology from a place of cultural homogeneity, disembodiment, domination, and hierarchy.

The original ethos of the Mobius Collective was to devise a space that simultaneously prioritized and centered healing practices for Mobius's members and emphasized the development of technological foundations, hardware, and software that would support the development of Liberatory Technology products. However, we quickly found that centering our own healing and embodying liberatory relationships was the only viable path forward to truly reflect loving-awareness-in-action as a direct manifestation of social justice in the world. From our very first gathering with one another as members of a newly multiracial team, the organization began its decolonization process. We foregrounded a relational process to create a set of agreements that came to define the foundation upon which our process of healing has emerged. These agreements have continued to take shape in accordance with how we are moving at the speed of trust and loving relationships until this day. The agreements were called the "Living Agreements" to acknowledge that these agreements would shift and change to reflect the needs and lived experiences of the people who seek to make Mobius a home. The following is an abbreviated version of the agreements.[5]

Mobius Living Agreements

Healing, Justice, and Equity: Living in a culture of domination means that we have a lot of healing to do from the ways we have been harmed by white supremacy, patriarchy, capitalism, and heteronormativity. We conscientiously explore what it means to heal ourselves; to prioritize individual and collective well-being; to redistribute power among ourselves; and to continually develop an understanding of what it means to show up with integrity to these principles. We practice embodying these qualities because they live in and are expressed through the body.

Spirit Is an Integral Force: We hold that Spirit is present in however we wish to connect to and honor that which is greater than ourselves. Spirit is a collaborative force behind everything that we do. A person can make meaning of connecting with Spirit in many ways and we affirm the vast diversity of people's experiences.

Wholeness and Embodiment: In contrast to the dominant culture's emphasis on the thinking mind, we honor the whole person and the wisdom held in the body. We believe that slowing down to notice sensation enables us to avoid harm and promote healing.

Acknowledge Trauma and Emotions: All bodies carry stress and a legacy of intergenerational trauma. Emotions are one of the primary means by which we express what has meaning to us, how we wish to be seen, and what we need from those around us. Emotional reactivity is a normal result of stress and the pressure to perform or produce, especially in organizational contexts. At Mobius, we recognize that it is very important to create a safe and brave space where people can have their emotions and/or trauma recognized when they arise. By slowing down and naming what is arising, we can intentionally practice cultivating presence. This allows us to see and hear one another more fully and supports our holistic well-being.

Emergence and Engagement with Time: "Emergence is the way complex systems and patterns arise out of a multiplicity of relatively simple interactions."[6] In order to notice these patterns and cocreate with each other and with Spirit, we honor emergence. This requires us to hold relationships with time differently: some meetings require more fluidity and spaciousness whereas others need to be time-fixed. And doing all of this requires a good dose of grace and humor.

An Example of Rupture in an Organizational Setting

Sometimes, one of the only ways to move toward healing after a rupture has occurred in an organizational setting is to have the courage to directly name a harm that is being done. Without naming the harm, there is no possibility of moving toward healing-as-accountability—though it is also important to state that simply naming a harm in an organizational space is not enough to ensure that processes of healing will be prioritized or considered as valid by all members of that organization, including the leadership. So having a leadership structure that understands the importance of healing and well-being for the healthy interpersonal dynamics of an organization is essential to this kind of work being able to happen. After all, everyone carries some form of intergenerational trauma in their nervous systems from living within a hegemonic social structure. Therefore, instances of rupture, and particularly racialized rupture within a racialized sociocultural context, are inevitable.

Intention is also important to center healing in an organization. If the practice of naming harm is done with the intention of catalyzing healing, and this is prioritized as a part of the organizational structure, then healing as an accountability practice is much more likely to occur. It needs to be the intention of everyone involved in the rupture to commit to exploring healing as it pertains to the specific organizational context in which the harm occurred. So this practice of healing-as-accountability is not one size fits all. One process cannot necessarily be transported directly from one organization to another. However, we hope this chapter makes a contribution to the collective conversation about healing-as-accountability in response to organizational ruptures, and that perhaps in the future a more broadly applicable methodology might evolve.

This commitment to healing may be experienced as inconvenient when juxtaposed with the other strategic or financial priorities that an organization may have, and this is a very important tension to name, because that situation can present its own unique set of real challenges for those involved in the rupture, as well as for those who are indirectly affected. As the Black-identified members of Mobius, we are framing our experience of rupture within Mobius through the lens of our lived experiences within this unusual organizational space. We used our lived experiences as Black people in the US (which is unique from the experiences of Black people elsewhere within the African diaspora) to develop an understanding of what we thought healing-as-accountability would feel like in response to this very particular instance in time, situated within a very specific historical context that we will explore in the following pages.

Though the aforementioned Living Agreements were in place and in practice from the beginning of the decolonization process of Mobius, it is pertinent to state that at that time the team was still composed of a majority of white-bodied persons and two Black-identified team members. We believe that this ultimately contributed to an imbalance in the power dynamic of the team. The Black-identified team members experienced repeated and consistent instances of feeling silenced and undermined by white-bodied team members regarding our viewpoints about how best to move forward to develop the organization with an aligned social justice orientation. This feeling of being disregarded continued to the point where the liberatory frameworks for healing that we had designed prior to engaging in the Mobius space were not actually centered in the operation of the organization, even when we explicitly agreed for this to happen.

It feels pertinent here to state that the Black-identified team members come from an ancestral tradition within the Black community in the US of having been raised in social and cultural environments where embodying Black liberation was our cultural heritage from the time we were born. We were both raised by several generations of family members who were steeped in the historical tradition of Black liberation through their experiences of leadership navigating the civil rights movement, which set the foundation for many other groups of marginalized people to be able to argue successfully for their human rights.

We did not think that our ways of embodying liberation and centering the knowledge that came from our own lived experiences of decolonization were always considered to be valid when expressed in the Mobius environment. For example, calls to embody compassion by slowing down with our approach to time and scheduling, or naming experiences of microaggressions and asking for accountability, were sometimes treated as getting in the way of more important business-related priorities. Expressing that we have differing viewpoints on social justice and liberation from white-bodied team members because of our lived experiences of being Black was not always treated seriously or as though these viewpoints were valid. This quote from Zenju Earthlyn Manuel exemplifies, in part, the wound as well as the healing opportunity that the issues we faced as a team presented:

> If we have created "race," we are all involved in the lived experience of it, whether we individually view ourselves in terms of race or not. When we are treated by others or act ourselves with a consciousness of race, we can count on an impact of that consciousness in everyone we interact with. If oppression is a particular type of suffering for some, then it is a general type of suffering for all. Do we all acknowledge this suffering? No. Are we all tender, in the sense of wounded soreness to it? Because of the nature of our interrelatedness, the answer is yes ... So why can't we use it in the service of liberating action?[7]

Part of what is so astute about Zenju's statement is that all of us were suffering in this context due to the negative impact of racialization and hierarchy in the Mobius space. This type of suffering is a part of the embodied experience of the perpetuation of harm that gets in the way of our collective efforts to embody liberation. However, as Black people, our suffering was felt as a form of oppression that was a continuation of the oppression that our ancestors have faced, tying our experience to centuries of intergenerational trauma. In our opinion, the suffering of the white-bodied team members came in the form of enacting manifestations of domination in the context of our work relationship, in spite of having the intentions to do the opposite. This example illustrates the difference between intent and impact when it comes to instances of racialized harm. These two types of suffering have very different impacts and consequences for people from different racialized identities. We believe that what happened during the Mobius rupture is a direct instance of how historical and intergenerational traumas can play out in an organizational context in a manner that reflects racialized suffering and harm.

Navigating the aforementioned tension of white supremacy culture came to a head during the aftermath of the white supremacist massacre of ten Black people in Buffalo, New York, in 2022. We want to name that this instance of racist violence was one of the most devastating hate crimes that this nation has ever experienced, and it also occurred against the backdrop of regular instances of police brutality and the death of unarmed Black people that has played out in this nation since its inception. It was directly after this incident that one of the Black team members reached out for emotional and spiritual support from the entire Mobius team to help process the extraordinary grief of that moment, only to be told by one of the white-bodied team members that resource mobilization was more important than being supported in their grief. This instance of prioritizing productivity over compassion, empathy, and presence is an enactment of white supremacy culture and capitalism. This was experienced by the Black Mobius team members as a moment of profound emotional violence and did not embody the safety, respect, and loving-awareness that is built into the Living Agreements. The Living Agreements had been designed to uphold the dignity and spiritual integrity of the team, particularly in the face of the violence of white supremacy culture, and a work ethos driven by racialized capitalism, but as is demonstrated in this case study, having agreements in place within an organization is no guarantee that harms will be prevented from occurring.

This instance resulted ultimately in what we have come to call a *rupture*. This rupture is an emotionally and psychologically painful moment of disconnection when marginalized people working within the context of majority white-bodied organizations experience the replication of systems of oppression through relational acts of denial, violence, and erasure. Such rupture results in the marginalized person feeling it necessary not only to call attention to these phenomena for the sake of recalibrating a sense of safety and justice, but also to slow down the pace and intention of the labor being attended to in order to focus upon the sense of humanity, dignity, and interconnection that needs to be restored. The Black-identified team members of Mobius, upon experiencing the erasure of our needs for emotional security, called upon our white-bodied team members to recognize that we would no longer work inside an organization still operating with principles of white supremacy culture. Rather than receiving the situation as a life-or-death moment, the company chose to prioritize its business-as-usual fashion of working as the cost of our collective humanity. The following actions were taken by the Black team members as a call-to-action for healing-as-accountability.

We called for typical work streams to come to a halt. We called for a period of time—three months total—in which we could experience radical rest and a caucused space dedicated to our ability to gather and practice relational ritual and sense-making around how we understood ourselves to have been dehumanized and to determine from an autonomous place how we envisioned moving forward and healing together. In conversation together, we raised several primary questions: How then does an organization that has unconsciously been founded upon upholding white supremacy culture and yet seeks to decolonize do so in a way that centers the needs of marginalized peoples? How does our organization prioritize loving-awareness-in-action in order to embody the liberation and social justice that we seek to model for other organizations involved in similar work? How do we develop a model of accountability-through-healing that can be embodied on a moment-to-moment basis such that we are actually being the change that we wish to see in the world? Beyond this, how can the process of healing ourselves, as those who are creating/producing technology in the world, become integral to the process of developing technological foundations and technologies that liberate while simultaneously acknowledging the politics of power and hierarchy that exist between racialized groups in the US?

Beyond the actions taken by the two Black team members, it is important to note that two of the three white-bodied team members voluntarily decided to step away from the work entirely to release more funding from their work streams to directly support temporarily increasing the salaries of the Black team members as a form of reparations. The remaining white-bodied team member voluntarily decreased their salary for several months in order to also support this effort at reparations. These actions represent very concrete sacrifices of capital that were made by white-bodied team members to manifest their collective awareness of the harms that had occurred within this organizational context. This was also a conscientious attempt to offer a degree of symbolic rectification that recognized the historical harms that have occurred in the context of systemic racism between the white and Black communities, ones that were deeply endemic to the historical violence and racialized trauma that undergirded the motivation behind the massacre in Buffalo.

It is also important to note that this critical work of healing-as-accountability that we name in the remainder of this chapter was supported financially by the Robert Wood Johnson Foundation, as well as the Ford Foundation, with full awareness of our activities. This is worth noting as it is perhaps widely believed that slow work, embodiment, rest, spiritual restoration, and healing processes may not be considered valuable in the context of philanthropic support of nonprofit industries in their efforts to model the future of the work of accountability; this case study demonstrates otherwise. We fully recognize that this is an unusual level of support to be received in the nonprofit industry, but we hope that telling our story will motivate more stakeholders who operate from places of economic power in our society to be inspired to allocate capital for the purposes of healing-as-accountability in organizations doing the work of social justice.

Our Response to the Mobius Organizational Rupture

The following is a representation of the Black-identified team members' response to the rupture. Our response, as we have previously indicated, is emergent and continues to evolve as a manifestation of our lived experiences navigating the world as Black-identified liberatory technologists while we are involved in the cocreation of the Mobius organizational space.

The following is a distillation of critical reflections and decisions that we made in order to embody loving-awareness-in-action and to catalyze our own healing, engendering collective healing processes as a manifestation of healing justice.

First, we decided to ground in Indigenous West African knowledge about the development of community because the creation of Beloved Community rooted in the expression of Indigeneity was our initial aim as a contribution to the Mobius Collective, and both of us share an identity as Indigenous West African people. It seemed that the following practices would be an organic manifestation of the embodiment of our ancestral knowledge as we sought to shape a container of healing within which to better experience the fullness of our authentic selves. As such, we drew on a list of "The Characteristics of Community," from the book *Ritual: Power, Healing, and Community* by Malidoma Patrice Somé.[8] This includes the following:

Unity of Spirit: The community feels an indivisible sense of unity. Each member is like a cell in a body. The group needs the individual, and vice versa.

Trust: Everyone is moved to trust everyone else by principle. There is no sense of discrimination or elitism. This trust assumes that everyone is innately well intentioned.

Openness: People are open to each other unreservedly. This means that individual problems quickly become community problems. Being open to each other depends upon trust.

Love and Caring: What you have is for everybody. There is a sense of sharing, which diminishes the sense of egoistic behavior. To have while others don't is an expression of you making up a society of your own.

Respect for the Elders: They are pillars and the collective memory of the community. They hold the wisdom that keeps the community together. They initiate the young ones, prescribe the rituals for various occasions, and monitor the dynamics of the community.

Respect for Nature: Nature is the principal book out of which all wisdom is learned. It is the place where initiation happens. It is the place from where the medicine comes. It nourishes the entire community.

Cult of the Ancestors: The ancestors are not dead. They live in the spirits of the community. They are reborn into the trees, the mountains, the rivers, and the stones to guide and inspire the community.

Healing-in-Community as Accountability

Significant healing arose between the Black team members of Mobius as we enacted and embodied the principles so beautifully articulated by Malidoma Patrice Somé. We met on a biweekly basis and openly discussed how our healing process could be framed by these principles individually and collectively. We engaged in practice around consciously naming and calling in our ancestors to each conversation in a way that acknowledges their aliveness, both in our bodies and in the earth. This allowed us to

171

discover how being in relationship with them catalyzed our healing of intergenerational trauma by connecting us to our ancestors as a source of power, affirmation, and dignity. We used somatic practices to feel into the degree to which we trusted one another from a place of embodied exploration; where there was mistrust or misalignment of intention toward one another, we named the sensations in our bodies that characterized this mistrust. We then went on to discuss this with the intention of reorienting profoundly toward trust in ourselves and each other. These conversations required incredible commitment to openness, love, and caring to make apparent to one another a sense that we desire to radically share resources, whether emotional/psychological or financial. We regularly turned toward the knowledge of elders in our families and communities to infuse our environment and way of being with their intuitive knowing. This part of our healing process was nothing short of extraordinary. All of the aforementioned represent only a portion of what it meant to heal together and elucidate part of how we arose into an empowered space from the place of the rupture.

The following statements are a sample of the realizations about what healing-as-accountability might look like in practice in an organizational setting, or a model of how-we-be or the being-with-ness with one another that is an extension of our desire to embody loving-awareness-in-action. They are a result of the learnings that occurred from our dedicated time to caucus and witness one another in our healing. We want to emphasize that these statements have also been written intentionally to be a form of lovingly disruptive prose, in a deliberately more casual visual format, to indicate their positionality in the chapter as a part of freedom-prose and freedom-dreaming, forms of writing that Black people are familiar with so when we read them, they visually indicate the liberatory feelings and emancipatory processes of the authors themselves. These reflections (and inquiries) arose from the process of the Black-identified team members' work to operationalize both the Mobius Living Agreements and Somé's "Characteristics of

Community," as outlined earlier, in the course of our process of relational repair:

- As above, so below—if there is illness in the root then illness will come out.

- True community does not start as somehow external to ourselves; community is a feeling that emerges from intentional inner processes that are deeply connected to a spiritual understanding of the feeling of the embodiment of interdependence.

- Healing is not about reform—the reforming of a paradox. Paradox is inherent in the process of healing:

  - A healing process is about how we are holding the balance of opposites rather than how we are exhibiting control.

  - Are we open and connected to one another as extended parts of self? How do we identify when the space is or is not reflecting this feeling back to us?

  - How are we being in remembrance of the vital importance of trust in one another by remembering ourselves as whole together?

  - When we allow ourselves to be whole together, we are tending to a garden rather than forcibly shaping it. We are not making the world into a process of mirroring our liking and preferences; rather, we are tending to the bond that is there.

- Use of intentional language. Do the words we use perpetuate old ways of being or lay the foundation for the new way of being that aligns with loving-awareness-in-action?

- We acknowledge that how we show up in any given moment is a manifestation of perfection even in its imperfection because we've treated perfection as a process and not a result (even imperfections can be revelations, or data that is relevant to how we experience self as it is evolving).

- The process of recognizing, witnessing, and reflecting wholeness to one another is integral to healing.

- We acknowledge that patterns of behavior get perpetuated when we treat people we deem to be flawed as needing to be stripped of their imperfections and that this is the manifestation of a type of psychological and structural violence.

    - Therefore, people need to be in spaces where they can come to know that nothing is wrong with them; we have to surrender judgment in order to allow our perception of ourselves and our environment to reflect wholeness.

- We are intentionally engaging in slow work that supports a relational process of revealing who we are to one another.

    - *Slow work* is a type of movement that is a manifestation of loving-awareness-in-action and the ways in which the violence of internalized capitalism and patriarchal norms urges us to move ever faster in the service of producing, rather than being and cocreating.

- We are getting to know one another in order to trust one another.

- Our slowing down to listen to really understand one another has been needed to know who we are, where we are coming from, and where we are going individually and together.

- We have leaned into the lessons of wisdom surrounding shared prosperity systems such as "Where the individual flourishes, so does the collective." This approach has yielded realizations that one person's growth is another person's growth in the context of community. The organic next step has been to be invested in both "our" (the individual self's) own growth and "our" (the all or collective's) growth.

- We are intentional in starting off meetings by feeling into our internal state of mind and being while sharing whatever we are present with.

- We trust that whatever we are present to in the moment, and are vulnerable enough to share—whether it is about what is happening in our personal or in our professional spheres—is what is of the essence in that moment and what resonates with the values of the "work" stream or the sacred labor.

- We engage in deep full-body listening and express patience with the flow of time in the space.

  - We engage in relational healing where we practice radical trust while revealing the work to one another.

  - How we move together in vulnerability matters in how it reveals subconscious concepts that we are dealing with.

  - We notice when we are moving at different paces (among ourselves) and reflect that back to one another in the spirit of loving-awareness in a manner that allows us to recognize difference and acknowledge the multiplicity of being.

  - We notice what our individual and collective relationship to time is—to being in new spaces with new people.

  - If we don't meet a certain timeline that we have set for ourselves, grace is the only thing that allows us not to go into a space of shame/blame/tension or aggression.

  - The way that we relate to both silence and speech is important in the space. It allows us room to understand, digest, process, metabolize, and reflect on thoughts, ideas, and embodiment so that they can evolve and we can create the conditions for new meaning-making.

- Integration (inner piece) + implementation (the application) of healing information are processes unto themselves.

  - We are creating, modeling, and embodying the conditions with which we might heal ourselves.

- It is important to recognize that what we are modeling for one another is not our learned behavior; it is not what we grew up in or what we have been previously acculturated to believe is normal behavior, and this needs to be openly acknowledged and celebrated.

- We are inundated by the media as well as religious, educational, governmental, and institutional authorities that attempt to define what culture is for us (so the context in which we are creating is in many ways antithetical to what we have experienced).

- We are in this overcoming or unlearning of entire states of being amid a greater macrocosm of culture and a world that does not reflect our processes back to us.

- The practice of acknowledging one another's divinity *simply because we exist* is also integral to this process of unlearning, and it undergirds our practice of accountability/reconciliation/repair.

- We acknowledge that people have different bodily rhythms and ways of moving through the world depending on their embodied and neurological identities.

  - People have different sensory capabilities that need to be considered of value rather than as deficits.

  - This acknowledges neurodiversity and the spectrum of dis/ability in the collective space as well.

- We acknowledge that we are living in an energetic world (a world made of energy) and that these energies, whether they are visible or not, affect us.

  - Doing this slow work together gives us the opportunity to notice and work with these energies, to love one another more deeply and feel into the complexity of what can be learned by revealing ourselves to one another with an intentional spirit of curiosity that allows us to rediscover our perfection.

- There is a flow to the practice and experience of opening up the mind and the heart—the way that we are both sensing and becoming conscious of the world around us.

- Trust, surrender, and openness are practices that are required when you are engaging people who are close to you in new spaces with different environments and languages.

- Choice becomes practice and practice becomes discipline (which is a practice employed within educational spheres, or places of learning new ways of sharing information and of being in relationship with one another).

- Focus (energy goes where attention flows), our intention of embodying loving-awareness as we move through the complexity of naming pain and injustice, informs our attention and therefore creates the conditions to return to love as our primary motivator for the sacred labor in which we are engaged.

Conclusion

Michael E. Gerber states in *The E-Myth Revisited*, "Your business is nothing more than a distinct reflection of who you are. If your thinking is sloppy, your business will be sloppy. If you are disorganized, your business will be disorganized . . . So if your business is to change—as it must continuously to thrive—you must change first. If you are unwilling to change, your business will never be capable of giving you what you want."[9] Further, ancient Kemetic wisdom states reflexive principles to this: "as above, so below." We even see this mirrored in biblical scriptural wisdom when it's noted that a tree is known by its fruit. With these understandings, we can know that our products, solutions, and processes are a natural offspring of how we are being. As such, at Mobius, we are operating with the innerstanding that the most fundamental shifts come when we look at ourselves deeply, grow in our self-awareness, and practice accountability to our aspirational values so that we might truly align with them.

From this, we can know that the outer results will resemble the same inner work that we have done. It is true and a common saying in the world of Western therapy that hurt people hurt people. In fact, when someone experiences a trauma that goes unhealed or unmetabolized, it multiplies the likelihood that they will cause someone else the same trauma. On the flip side, though, Mobius is testing the theory that, conversely, healed people can heal people, healed systems can heal systems, and so on. We are the practicing embodiment of giving ourselves permission to truly acknowledge all our traumas and embrace them with loving arms so that we can heal them, so we do not let them leak, unattended to, into the fruits we bear. Though we experienced a rupture in the Mobius team that reflected the pain of systemic oppression on a macro level, within our microcosm of relationality, through grounding in ancestral wisdom and applying the Living Agreements of how we be together, we were able to attune to ways of being that engendered our capacity to orient around healing as the primary lens through which we perceive and enact our capacity to heal, and therefore be accountable to one another. We are, in effect, tilling our own soils/souls and planting the seeds into our soil as a way to cultivate healthy foundations that can produce technological fruit that fully aligns with the healed and free world we wish to coexist in together.

Several specific points can be made here in terms of how it is that we managed to keep up this level of collective healing, interpersonal awareness, and relationship fostering while also attending to the goals and to-do items that were expected of us by funders. As stated previously, we spent a period of time that lasted several months moving at the speed of trust and carefully attuning to each other's hearts, minds, and day-to-day experiences of healing. Eventually, we were able to determine that we were ready to begin to shift our conversations to hold more of a balance between emphasizing healing-in-community and orienting around what needed to be done to articulate our new organizational structure and our aims for what we sought to produce in the world. We were willing to feel into renegotiating the nonlinear rhythm and flow of being emergent and deeply relational, while pivoting toward attending to matters of deadlines and resource mobilization by sensing into which of these aspects needed greater attention on a given day, week, or month. We continually understand that life is always shifting and changing and calling for a different pace and tempo of labor. It may be that the extremely small size of our team after the rupture helped this radical slowing-down to happen. We recognize that the ways in which we were supported in this process of embodying healing-as-accountability were totally rare and extraordinary. We wish that was not the case and are actively seeking to understand how we might contribute to the development of a liberatory tech ecosystem in which the type of support we received becomes more equally distributed in organizations that are in desperate need of it.

We returned to our original goal of stewarding and developing liberatory tech products, this time centering on understanding how to merge the liberatory frameworks (see Davion "Zi" Ziere's Liberatory Tech Foundations)[10] and technology (see Sará King's Systems-Based Awareness Map [SBAM])[11] that each Black team member had originally intended to have centered in the space. For instance, Mobius began to actively steward the launch of the SBAM, the world's first 3D interactive AI-integrated map of human awareness. The SBAM software is being developed to show the relationship between internal and external awareness as they relate to the healing of intergenerational trauma and the development of well-being. The software creates beautiful data visualizations that show the relationship between language-based data (what people report from their lived experiences using voice or text) and biometric data from wearables to capture our unique daily journey toward well-being, which together clearly show areas of growth and deliver personally tailored recommendations that encourage the development of healing and loving-awareness individually and collectively. Importantly, the SBAM celebrates and centers intersectional identity and highlights the mapping of intergenerational trauma in its measurement of well-being, creating a liberatory technology that prioritizes the experiences of those who are affected by systemic oppression and marginalization each day, while demonstrating or suggesting potential healing pathways forward. The SBAM is being designed to incorporate the Liberatory Tech Foundations, outlining the underlying frameworks and protocols for Liberatory Technology, as well as the community, trust, and equity model for sustainable, shared prosperity and holistic well-being. We have built the capacity to focus our energy on developing the Liberatory Technology ecosystem and broader community, along with creating the support structure for this specific technology to be created because of our efforts to center healing-as-accountability first and foremost.

Though as a team we have shifted into greater emphasis on organizational development and financial sustainability, we continue to do our very best to embody the Living Agreements by a) continuing to practice slowing down our movements and conversations to allow for greater spaciousness; b) attuning to and acknowledging the importance of consciously remembering to breathe deeply with one another; c) grounding in embodiment and meditation practices before beginning any to-do-related conversation (and really throughout any conversation in order to connect with Spirit); d) noticing when we might be stepping outside of alignment with agreed-upon values so that we might realign together, whether via understanding or accountability; and e) centering Indigenous knowledge, healing practices, and the earth as our partner in co-constructing our ways of knowing and being in the world, including in every decision that gets made. *This is by no means an exhaustive list of our practices together*, but it does give a few examples that other organizations can easily take up that are interested in shifting how they be together. Notably, this was slow work. Altogether, this process of healing has taken place across the time span of a year; organizations seeking to experiment with their own processes should note that what we have written about here is no quick-fix because what we have described is moving at the speed of trust, rather than at the speed of capitalism.

In a sense, it is challenging to describe or convey exactly how we knew when trust had been rebuilt between us, other than that as practitioners of healing and embodiment, we trusted our nervous systems to tell us when peace was being experienced between us; when we experienced being at rest with one another; the restoration of loving and nonviolent communication; the departure of emotional reactivity in our relating to one another; and the presence of compassion, empathy, and belonging that felt authentic and real to each member. Then we knew the feeling of radical trust had been reestablished and that every aspect of our work would arise from this space of embodied knowing. The feelings that we are describing might not be experienced the same by those who read this and are undergoing similar processes and experiences. What the restoration of trust feels like in one group might not feel the same subjectively to another. If a group or organization is going through an experience of a rupture and does not have access to practitioners of embodiment, somatic, or contemplative practices rooted in social justice who can hold space for compassionate healing-as-accountability, then we very strongly recommend investing in such access.

We feel as though we have modeled healing-as-accountability together (though we recognize that this is continual life work) for several different reasons. Somatically, or in our mind-body connection, we can sense that the hierarchy, domination, violence, trauma, and general energy of misunderstanding that used to exist between us is no longer there. The quality of our interpersonal connection is one of calm, peaceful connectedness, compassion, empathy, forgiveness, spaciousness, and communication that feels transparent and open-hearted. We continue to recognize and name the ways in which our differing social locations and intersectional identities mean that we have different experiences of power and advantage or disadvantage in the world. What this means is that the values of the dominant culture will, on occasion, still arise in our dynamics. When this happens, we must engage in a process of truth-telling, but when we do this from a place of embodiment, compassion, and centering loving-awareness, as well as with humility on the part of those who may be unconsciously enacting domination, we can continue to reorient ourselves toward our stated goals. We practice openness about how power differences in society might be showing up in our organizational dynamics, but we name this in a way that prioritizes nonviolent, loving communication and total trust; ultimately, we love and wish to whole-heartedly support one another. We feel it is of great importance to regularly express our love and affirmation of one another so that it is heard, felt, and received.

Embodying dedicated, unconditional love in the context of an organization might be one of the most radical ways in which we can heal together. It requires extraordinary commitment. There is a feeling of real community, of being family, between us, and this feels precious considering the heart-level fragmentation, violence, and division we are aware of broadly in society. We are doing our very best to completely trust that the energy of our hearts and loving-awareness as a field of being tell us when we are in balance and when we tend to our misalignment. We are each dedicated to our own individual healing outside of the organizational context, and we take the time to share with one another actively what practices we are engaged in and what we are learning from them. Though we know that this healing process that we are describing may look different in every organization, we remain overjoyed that we have experienced the healing that we have been able to authentically touch into and sincerely hope that others are able to model and articulate their own ways of embodying loving-awareness-in-action inside of an organization, and into the world.

9

BUILDING TRANSFORMATIVE MOVEMENTS

Deep Democracy and Beloved Community

Taj James and Beloved Communities Network

Now is a time of great transition and change. Around the globe, we see unprecedented climate disruption and upheaval across economic, political, and cultural systems. We see people—entire populations—facing this great, unknowable landscape and seeking paths to a future they can believe in.

In this time, we also feel a calling, an invitation, a possibility, beyond what we can presently observe, and we see this calling reflected across powerful emerging movements.

Now is a time of risk and danger, but it's also a time of opportunity: a chance to transform our local and global communities. We have the capacity to answer this call. We have the capacity to bring forth a future that is struggling to be born. We have the capacity to be the future we long for, to be the power and strength of our vision, our purpose, and our relationships.

Our movements are demanding that we recognize the ways in which we've become numb, silent, complacent, or complicit in accepting the unacceptable. Our movements are calling on us to acknowledge and honor our mutual vulnerability and undeniable interdependence. Our movements want more than access to the powers that be; they want to generate new forms of power. Our movements are calling on us to make a courageous commitment to love.

This is the calling Beloved Communities Network seeks to nurture and amplify. Beloved Communities Network cultivates changemakers: People who dare to rise to the challenges facing humanity.[1] People who see the potential for transformation and are working to make it real. People who understand the present moment and are poised to make change as leaders of powerful movements. This lies at the core of Beloved Communities Network's purpose: to nurture whole people and whole communities to transition from a world of domination and extraction to a world of regeneration, resilience, and interdependence; to embody *Love, Care, and Community*.

The Practices of Transformative Movements

Leading with bold vision and purpose, movement builders are moving beyond the question of "What do we need to do?" to ask, "Who do we need to be and what do we need to embody together to bring forth the transformation we seek?"

In this way, our movements are learning the art of time travel; starting by visioning the future we want, we are accelerating change by embodying and manifesting the values we seek in the world, right here and right now. We are not just asking people to believe another world is possible; we are inviting all of us to generate and experience a new world through transformative practice and strategy.

Transformative movements recognize that we are connected as whole people and whole communities. Because our issues and problems are systemic and interconnected, our solutions and movements must be as well. The challenges we face swell from a deep reservoir of historical and social forces. Our approach must match the depth of the challenge with a depth of practice and strategy. We must meet depth with depth.

Our Journey to Meet the Moment

Our growing movements for social and ecological justice are in a very different place now than they were a few decades ago. Back in the early '90s, a generation of young adults (who had been children of members of the diverse movements for justice of the early '70s) were looking for ways to carry forward those traditions and continue the work of social change. At that time, we were faced with a social change ecosystem that was deeply fragmented and divided; we were clear about what we were fighting against but had no compelling vision of the world we wanted to build. Because we were reactive and defensive, angry, and self-righteous about the injustice in the world, the ways we were going about our efforts reflected more of the fear and desire for control and domination at the heart of the extractive system than the love our ancestors had passed down to us.

One consequence of this was that we were "winning" our campaign and changing policies, but despite that, the well-being of our people and the planet was not improving. We were losing ground. Movement leaders began to grapple and search for a different path forward. Some of us came together at that time to create the Movement Strategy Center to cultivate space to explore the core question of how our ways of building power could reflect the values at the heart of our transformative vision. The insights shared here emerged from the Transitions Labs and Beloved Communities Network that grew from space the Movement Strategy Center created to explore those questions. This is the story of an evolution of transformational movement building and how many streams, leaders, and organizations evolved the field.

The story of the Beloved Communities Network and the broader transformational change movement is a story of reclamation, renewal, and remembrance; a return to source and to the core of our humanity; the restoration of a spirit-centered life, rooted in ancient spiritual and Indigenous wisdom practices; and a fierce commitment to transcend the false choices of the binary culture that kept us trying to dismantle the master's house through an inversion of the master's mindset.[2] A growing network of changemakers has begun to recognize that we shape change at the broadest structural levels in every small choice we make. The network is a mycelial tapestry of listening, healing, courage, care, and creativity, movement by movement, and day by day.

Healing is both individual and collective.
And through healing, we reconnect to the individual and collective
power that structural violence has disconnected us from.

Insights from Future Stories

In 2014, the Movement Strategy Center gathered movement leaders to explore the ways that embodied wisdom could generate untapped possibility, potential, and power in the work toward social, economic, and ecological justice. Over three hundred movement leaders from across the country took part in these gatherings, with experiences that have rippled out into innovation far beyond our wildest dreams. Over this last decade, these leaders have expanded their practices into the networks, alliances, and coalitions they are leading across communities, sectors, and movements to build a shared vision, align communities, and advance a movement of movements of "10,000 Beloved Communities."[3]

The engine behind this work is the shared exploration of unifying and catalyzing questions. Our founding question continues to serve as a powerful compass:

How do we transition from a world of domination and extraction
to a world of regeneration, resilience, and interdependence?

This question has shaped everything about the work we've done together, turning our gatherings into labs where leaders could try out audacious vision, embodiment, radical connection, and strategic navigation, then go back out into movements to test them, and stay in a learning community with people across the country who are innovating, too. Through collective physical practice, we cultivated spaciousness, energy, rhythm, and resonance that allowed us to interrupt old habits and transcend limiting mindsets so that we could dream of new ways forward, forge broader and deeper relationships, and develop new projects that would help us to transform our communities.

Inspired by environmental justice leaders who were advancing just transitions from an extractive to a regenerative economy centered in sacredness, we began to focus on cultivating the spiritual grounding and power shifting practices at the heart of movement work. We intentionally brought leaders from diverse movement sectors beyond ecological justice into the unifying work of advancing holistic transitions and futurist imaginings. One way we did this was through our core practice of Future Stories where we imagine a future descendant writing a letter of gratitude to their ancestors from one hundred years back describing the future they are thriving in and what had to happen over those years for that reality to come into being. This includes describing the obstacles that were overcome and the key leaps, pivots, and breakthroughs that disrupted the cycle of incremental change and turned impossible challenges into inevitable victories.

Out of those vision stories came projects like Parenting for Liberation, created by a leader in the movement to end gender-based violence who struggled with the question of how to parent her Black son in ways that did not seek to keep him safe by insisting that the fear in his body was the only thing protecting him from the anti-Black violence of the state.[4] The vision and breakthrough emerged by creating the space to find and sit with the question of how to parent a Black boy from a place of love and liberation beyond fear.

Future Story practice created space to see beyond the fear and pain that had left generations of Black parents feeling like we need our children to feel pain and fear to keep them from being killed by the police or harmed in other ways by a system that continues to work toward our extermination. As a parent of Black children, I was so grateful that someone took on the work to help us move beyond the collective survival responses that have kept us alive but at the price of our tender hearts.

This kind of work was also an interruption of an old social change habit that saw power building and systems change work as being solely about the work of political organizing and campaigning that created policy change but did not view the work of care and community as core to cultural and systems transformation. Seeing the work of collective human development and the cultivation of community as foundational to broader cultural and systems transformation was the core wisdom insight at the heart of our labs process and network.

The Beloved Communities Network emerged with relationships, visions, strategic collaborations, projects, and ideas unfolding across places and networks. The Transitions Labs made a valuable and lasting contribution to transformative movement building in multiple ways, growing waves of leaders who shift culture and systems with the extraordinary depth, boldness, vision, and strategy this moment in human history so urgently needs. Transitions Labs created space for movement leaders to listen to the wisdom in their bodies, to practice, and to embrace the reminder from Hawaiian elder and Zen teacher Norma Wong that any strategy we engage in today has been shaped by (at least) the hundred years before us and must be accountable to those who will be here (at least) one hundred years from now.[5]

Within the community's one-hundred-year vision, we understand that this is a pivotal cultural moment in history that will significantly shape how children, families, and communities see themselves and the meaning of the future. The story of how we see ourselves shapes how we feel about and engage with present-day democratic processes, how and whether we engage in the deeper project of collective self-determination, and how we understand ourselves in relationship to generations to come.

A New Way: Four Elements of Transformative Movements

Like many kindred movement makers, Beloved Communities Network believes incremental change strategies are increasingly inadequate in the face of rapidly accelerating climate disruption and growing inequality. Incremental change strategies cannot keep pace. Because the scale and nature of the problems we face are exponential, our change strategies need to be exponential as well. We need transformative strategies to generate exponential change. And as movement leader Ai-jen Poo of the National Domestic Workers Alliance reminds us, transformative change starts "from the bottom up and from the inside out."[6] If we want the world to transform, we have to begin with ourselves and our closest relationships and, when seeking solutions, focus on the people and communities closest to the challenge.

But how do we accomplish this? How do we achieve transformation—the exponential shift of reality? Beloved Communities Network recognizes four elements at the core of transformative movement building: leading with audacious vision and bold purpose; deeply embodying the values at the heart of the vision; building radical connection and deep community around the vision; and using all of that—vision, embodiment, and connection—to strategically navigate toward the future. By traveling the paths at the intersection of our power and pain, we can make new ways forward into a thriving future.

Creating spaces to practice these four elements, like we do in Transitions Labs, is critical. Doing so cultivates a fertile soil that, if cared for with love, will nurture the seeds and sprouts of a hopeful future allowing it to take root, grow, evolve, and spread. Such fertile soil literally grounds people in their purpose, inspires them to believe in their vision, and offers them space to practice navigating toward an achievable horizon of transformation.

1. Leading with Audacious Vision and Bold Purpose

When the Beloved Communities Network started our work, we learned to ask questions to confront change efforts that were isolated, fragmented,

189

and often unaligned in order to help develop a broader vision; for example: What are we fighting for and working to build? How are our various efforts related? What are the deeper structures underlying the problems we're working on? Who else shares our affinity and purpose? What visions and purposes do we share?

Transformative movement builders are guided by a vision that is audacious and bold enough to unite diverse movements in building the world we need. This vision is not utopic, not a yearning for the impossible. Nor is it nostalgic, harkening back to something that never existed. Transformative movement builders imagine the path forward to possible futures we cannot yet grasp. We lead others to share in this vision and contribute to a larger purpose. Our dreams are rooted in the wisdom of the past, with awareness of the present, and hope for the future.

Whether it is the visionary work of activists in the Resonance Network who are working toward a world of peace and safety beyond gender-based violence, or the transformative vision of the Climate Justice Alliance to advance a just transition to a local, living economy that centers the sacred, transformative movements are reaching back to reclaim ancestral wisdom and are embodying the love, care, and community that is helping make transformative visions feel not just possible, but inevitable. Communities are asking themselves what their seven-generation dreams are for a thriving future for their grandchildren's grandchildren and narrating one-hundred-year visions.[7]

Communities in Richmond, California, are providing us with a vibrant example of how to lead with audacious vision and bold purpose. They are imagining (and advancing) a local, thriving economy where the oil refinery at the heart of their community that has polluted the land and poisoned the people for decades has been replaced and the harm that has been done has been repaired by creating a vibrant, biodiverse, food-rich local economy that is an anchor for generating economic solutions to advance climate resilience and community prosperity. This models for us how, at the heart of this proactive work, we not only travel into the future, but also backward-map the milestones and leaps in our capacity and the pivots in our strategy that we will need moving forward from the present.

2. Deep Embodiment

The dominant cultural separation of mind, body, and spirit contributed to a justice movement culture that led many of us to try to think and talk our way to a different future. Too often, transformation was only reality in our own minds. The recognition, reclamation, and renewed reverence for the body has been key to a renewed somatic approach to transformation. *Believing* another world is possible is different from *practicing* another world in our daily lives. Transformative movement builders are learning to step into the future, *generating and experiencing* a new world here and now by practicing and embodying a new set of values. Embodiment is re-membering and re-rooting in the today.

Transformative movement builders recognize that patterns of injustice are maintained through repeated day-to-day actions. Taking on injustice requires conscious practices that create new forms of culture and new modes of relating to ourselves and to each other. These practices emphasize mutual interdependence and care between individuals and groups, communities, and the planet. Beyond working against injustice, transformative movement builders work for liberation. We must do this by developing creative, innovative practices of liberation, from the micro to the macro levels. We must commit to cultivating new ways of being, defined by joy, humor, and humility; we must step into the fullness of our responsibility to ourselves and each other, with love. We must recognize that the secret is *to be the future now, to "be what happens next"* instead of trying to predict and control what happens in the future.

Core to embodiment is approaching life as practice, recognizing that as individuals, organizations, communities, and movements, we have been shaped, and that to reshape ourselves, we must engage in conscious collective practice and rituals that help us to interrupt the unconscious habits of our old shapes. These old shapes no longer serve us to cultivate

191

the gifts, strengths, capacity, and qualities that we need to uncover within ourselves to bring our full power to bear in service of our purpose.[8]

For some leaders, the move toward embodiment was an affirmation that centering spirit and healing work in our change efforts was the key to making transformative leaps. For instance, Alexis Flanagan of the Resonance Network claims,

> In centering spirit I've expected pushback and resistance and critique, but instead the response has been an overwhelming affirmation of how much this is wanted and needed. People want to think about what it means to connect to something bigger; to make visible the way that movement works, ancestrally and currently, has always been spirit led. I saw this in a recent statewide conference in Idaho where there was a plenary on how we engage spirit and ancestors in movement work— and 150 people went to the breakout session afterward.[9]

Other leaders in the Beloved Communities Network integrated their embodiment practices with their transformational vision work to shift their political stance from a reactive to a proactive one. With the benefit of knowing what your community needs for future generations, different solutions in the present become visible. Maria Ibarra-Frayre of We the People Michigan described her experience in this way:

> Practicing embodying our vision has made us less reactive. When we feel aligned with our breath and grounded in our bodies, it's much easier to be proactive and creative, not just backed into a corner in defense mode.[10]

This approach to embodiment leads activists and organizations to not simply turn to spiritual and therapeutic healing and embodiment practices, but to make a return to sound, song, breath, movement, and martial traditions as ways to embed practices of breath, energy, resonance, and rhythm.

These core embodiment practices are rooted in the ancient wisdom of all intact cultural communities: that to use our hands together, to breathe and sing and move together, to *be* and cocreate in community together, are how we become a "bigger we" that invites all people into the circle of belonging, care, and collaboration. Embodiment practice in movements has been about reclaiming the core cultural wisdom of the community and infusing that back into the colonial confines of the nonprofit industrial complex and anger-centered reactionary left and labor movements. In our labs, we use our hands to build things, we rest and reflect, we move together in a ten-step Tai Ji form created for movement organizations, but most importantly, we breathe together, resonate together, and sing together.

In many movement organizations you go to today, it is not unusual to take collective deep breaths before going into the context of the meeting. Or to start the meeting with a song. That was not true in the late '90s when many of us began moving our work this direction. Breathing and moving in rhythm literally aligns our heartbeats and when we do that first, before tackling a tough challenge or trying to find a creative solution, we are able to bring unleashed clarity, focus, and creativity to our changemaking.

One of the communities that has deeply embraced the physical aspects of embodiment practice has been in the work of advancing climate justice. The People's Climate Innovation Center through their partnerships with Facilitating Power are the anchor partners in our community who bring the embodied Latin American wisdom of popular theatre to the Beloved Communities Network.[11] Through these practices, instead of simply talking and writing ideas on flip charts and whiteboards, the community creates tableaus and physical collective articulations of the problems they face and the solutions they seek. Without words and speaking only with bodies, stories are told, scenarios are developed, and strategic puzzles are solved. And as a result, communities find ways to finally shut down the polluting power plant in their neighborhood or win the transfer of land back to the community so they can grow the food that is needed to feed the people. The wisdom that emerges from collective and creative embodiment practices supports our communities to accomplish things they could not have imagined otherwise and find more direct ways to accelerate the implementation of their solutions.

3. Radical Connection and Community

Transformative movements recognize that everything gets done through relationships and nothing gets done without them. This fundamental truth reflects an ecosystem approach that is based in interdependence and interconnectedness. Movements are about people and cultures, our relationships to each other, and our relationship to the planet. Bringing movements into alignment with each other is not about making others fall into line or replacing one vision with another. It is about cultivating a bigger sense of movement, recognizing and acting on connections that already exist. It is about cocreating a story of the future and inviting others to engage in advancing it. It is about resonating and connecting with one another. It is about healing and generating new life-affirming possibilities together. Through deep listening, breakthrough conversations, and the cultivation of radical connections, movements can make leaps that were previously unthinkable.

For decades the work of Movement Strategy Center was focused on building networks and alliances that could help us to build enough *integrated,* spiritual, cultural, political, and economic power for new worlds to emerge.[12] Those leaders who had been working to recenter practice in their own lives and organizations began to bring those approaches into the network and alliances they were building.

These were leaders who had already built networks bringing together thousands of leaders and hundreds of organizations, but in the space we created of Transitions Labs, they built a depth of connection and space to practice a process that helped them think about their work in a radically deeper way. They were then able to return to their own organizations and networks, facilitate greater community connections, and build upon the networks they had cultivated in the labs to advance this movement of movements. The transformative movement building then began to move from the margins to the center of progressive social movements.[13]

Trina Greene Brown, from Parenting for Liberation, shared that "In the lab we focused on shifting to what we are saying yes to. How to move from no to yes has been a fundamental question for me."[14] Building alignment around our "Shared Yes!" and common vision, around what we are for and not just what we are against, is critical to building the "big we" needed for transformation to be possible.

4. Strategic Navigation

With audacious vision, deep embodiment, and radical connection, transformative movement builders can strategically adapt to and navigate rapidly changing environments. Strategic navigation requires new forms of leadership that transcend traditional modes of domination. From whatever position we hold, transformative movement builders must be leaders for the whole, bringing people together with a bigger purpose in mind. We must cultivate a thorough understanding of systems and forces in motion—the general operating conditions of our movements—and forge paths that get us where we need to go. Transformative movement builders foster collaborative action that is nonlinear, synergistic, and highly networked, finding multiple paths that are strategically differentiated but headed to the same mountain top. They have an understanding of the physics of movement building—kinetic and potential energy, resonance, critical mass, exponential scaling. They align different approaches into collective strategies that leverage everyone's strengths. This is what allows transformative movements to make big leaps toward a new society, even as they dismantle old systems that no longer serve us. From a position of collective power, strategic navigation guides us toward an emergent future.

Erin Dale, a healer and economic and political activist from The Partnership Fund in Durham, North Carolina, reflected on how a longer-term vision helped her to broaden and expand her strategic approach:

The labs invited me to think in terms of 100 years, to reflect on what I want my descendants to say about my work in 75 years. I think a lot about how we can develop the systems we need to feed, clothe, house, educate ourselves—to become self-sufficient—while simultaneously trying to impact electoral debate and hold electeds accountable.[15]

This holistic long-arc vision that Erin brought to her work led her to deepen her own offerings as a healing practitioner in her community, all the while leading a national collaborative that brings resources to grassroots political power building. And in recognizing the limits of traditional political organizing, she has also begun to grow from that parallel effort to build Black economic power by funding Black-led food and agriculture cooperatives across the country.

These strategies embody the recentering of healing and spirit work in political practice and regrounding ourselves in the restoration of our relationships to land and economic self-determination. The holistic and long-arc view, rooted in ecological and ancestral worldviews, has supported many spirit-centered transformational leaders to focus on building integrated cultural, political, and economic power that is essential for transformation.

Many other leaders in the Network are working to rematriate and return land, labor, capital, and creativity to community and the commons to build a foundation of economic self-determination that is foundational to liberation.[16] As our Movement Generation Justice and Ecology Project family reminds us, "What we do to the land, we do to the people. When we free the land, we free the people."[17]

Many leaders in the Network are land and water protectors and environmental justice leaders who have been defending their communities from extractive industries that poison the soil, air, and water and accelerate the climate crisis. In recent years, their communities have shifted their attention to land back and reparations efforts that rematriate land to Indigenous sovereignty to continue the work of cleaning up the impacts of our colonial economy to restore biodiversity, recapture carbon in the soil, and grow food to feed the people.

Many of these movement-based projects are also creating centers for practice, healing, renewal, and strategy. Some are ancestral homes on their tribal territories, others are in the foothills surrounding our urban centers, and others are partnering with Black farmers struggling to hold onto their land in the face of persistent and ongoing discrimination and pressure from large agribusiness. Reconnecting to place and repairing our relationships to the land are becoming even more critical as the impacts of climate chaos accelerate and fires, floods, heat waves, and hurricanes make our fragile and desecrated environment even more precarious.

Beloved Community is rooted in repairing relationships within the human family, but that is only possible when we repair our relationship to the land, water, Mother Earth, the web of life, and all our more-than-human relatives. Repairing our relationships to place is at the center of the work across the ten thousand Beloved Communities. And it is how we restore holistic balance and grounding to the movement work of power building and transformation.

Practicing into the Future Now

Transformational movements connect us with ourselves, each other, and with the whole—the whole of our communities, the whole of humanity. Transformational movements affect all levels of our experience: the way we think, our structures and systems, the way we live, and even who we are. Through the practices of leading with vision, deep embodiment, radical connection, and strategic navigation, movement makers transform ourselves, our movements, our strategies, our relationships, and our world. We can identify the unconscious habits and patterns of behavior that limit our communities' ability to recognize our full power and potential. And we can develop new practices and strategies to do what was previously impossible. Together we can transition from a world where the few live at the expense of the many to a world where the many govern for the benefit of all. As many movements are saying, we need all of us to change everything.

Using the Four Elements to Build Deep Democracy and Beloved Community

In this moment we are asking: How do we use the attacks against us to leap forward toward a liberatory vision? How do we seize this moment to build the depth of transformative solutions that will allow us to weather the storms ahead while also bringing to life the new world that is emerging from the bottom up? How do we make the big transition we need to nurture whole people and whole communities and to transition from a world of domination and extraction to a world of regeneration, resilience, and interdependence?

For a long time, our movements felt stuck in a binary: is it more important *first* to build power to change conditions that create individual and systemic harm or to heal from the past and current impacts of those systems so we can reclaim the power we need to change systems? The Deep Democracy work—the combination of healing and wholeness, community voice and power, repairing structural harm and governing for the whole—that the Network engaged in in the labs was a way to grapple with this false binary and find a way forward that affirmed that we must simultaneously work at the intersection of our power and pain, individually *and* collectively.[18] We must support healers, spirit doulas, cultural bearers, and our organizers and power builders and be in circle and community together.

Collectively practicing the four elements of transformative movements—vision, embodiment, connection, and navigation—is how we travel the two paths at the intersections of power and pain, healing, and cultural and systems transformation. It is a practice that moves us beyond the binaries of left and right to a way of being rooted in the wisdom of "inside out and bottom up."

In these times, our communities are exploring Deep Democracy, rooted in Beloved Community, as a way forward toward the emergent transition we need. Together we are exploring the practice of place that grounds us and nurtures our interdependence with each other and our Mother Earth. Together we are embodying vision and connection in times of uncertainty. Together we are exploring our seven-generation story of the future and the one-hundred-year arc of practice and strategy we are living into.

Working to embody the four elements as we travel the two paths is at the heart of the practice growing within the Beloved Communities Network. It brings together in deep collaboration those working on healing justice—starting with the impacts we experience at an individual and collective level and the healing work we must do to reclaim our individual and collective power that systemic harm and trauma severs us from—and those looking to mitigate the harm and build collective care beyond the systems and structures that reproduce that violence and harm. Weaving the work of healing and repair from the individual to the collective and back again is how we transcend the dualism of "me vs. we" in the practice of community.

While we do the *valley work* of healing individually and collectively from the past harm produced by systems of othering, violence, and domination, our communities are also doing the *mountain work* of reclaiming our individual and collective power, finding our voice to tell our stories and speak our truths in ways that reconnect across the divide-and-conquer rifts that have kept us apart and disconnected us from our collective power. In coming home to ourselves, and by reconnecting to the sacred responsibilities we hold as descendants of ancestors and ancestors of future descendants, we articulate the collective visions that are at the center of power we build to bring those visions to life in each and every moment.

> *Valley work is about healing from the past. Mountain work is the collective leadership work of creating a different future in the here and now. We build the future through the repair of the past. One, then the other. And both all at once.*[19]

This work reflects a movement within the human family to return to deep ancestral wisdom and repair our relationships to the web of life and

Mother Nature. Moving beyond the old "Lie of Separation, Supremacy, and Scarcity,"[20] recognizing that we are nature itself, seeing the harm that humans have done to humans over the last five hundred years and the last five thousand years, are leading to a return to the ways of being and ways of life that support creativity, joy, and thriving for the entire human family and all of our relations. Transcending the binaries that separate inner work and systems work and healing work from power shifting is the art of transformational practices.

The story of the development of the Beloved Communities Network is briefly summarized here but chronicled in greater detail in the series of reports and curriculum guides that contain the full stories from movement leaders about how they are bringing these principles and practices into their lives, communities, organizations, and movements.[21] One can get a flavor of the power of these approaches through reading these stories, though the power of this way forward can only be experienced in practice and community. Most of you reading this are likely already deeply practicing these principles in your own lives.

My two decades at Movement Strategy Center were about reclaiming and restoring *spiritual power* and ancestral and community wisdom in movements that were focused on *building political and cultural power*. In the Beloved Communities Network, I found a space where we get to continue to reclaim, balance, and reweave our wholeness. This work of grappling with the core transformative questions has since led me to leave my role at Movement Strategy Center to start a project called Full Spectrum so I can focus on supporting community stewards who are taking sacred responsibility for caring for their people and their place by building the community economic power and wealth that is foundational to just transitions.[22] The evolution of my own transformative practice continues alongside many other changemakers as we seek new ways to integrate cultural, spiritual, political, and economic power for our collective transformation.

The principles and practices are effective not because any of us created them, but because, as a community, we were able to recognize deeper truths about ourselves and the habits in the broader culture that we all have internalized by living in the toxic stew of the dominant culture and system. This path is one of many paths up the mountain and if it resonates with you, we encourage you to reflect on the questions we continue to grapple with as Beloved Communities and share the fruits of your practice and power with love.

Bibliography

Acosta, Angel. *Acosta Institute* (podcast). Produced by Angel Acosta. https://podcasts.apple.com/us/podcast/acosta-institute/id1629688914.

Ahmed, Sara. *Complaint!* Durham, NC: Duke University Press, 2021.

———. "Selfcare as Warfare." feministkilljoys. August 25, 2014. https://feministkilljoys.com/2014/08/25/selfcare-as-warfare/.

Akomolafe, Bayo. *These Wilds Beyond Our Fences*. Berkeley, CA: North Atlantic Books, 2017.

Alexander, M. Jacqui, Lisa Albrecht, Sharon Day, and Mab Segrest, eds. *Sing, Whisper, Shout, Pray! Feminist Visions for a Just World*. Fort Bragg, CA: EdgeWork Books, 2002.

American Civil Liberties Union. "Mapping Attacks on LGBTQ Rights in U.S. State Legislatures." Accessed August 1, 2023. https://www.aclu.org/legislative-attacks-on-lgbtq-rights.

Andreotti, Vanessa Machado de Oliveira. *Hospicing Modernity: Facing Humanity's Wrongs and the Implications for Social Activism*. Berkeley, CA: North Atlantic Books, 2021.

Angelou, Maya. "Dave Chappell + Maya Angelou." *Iconoclasts*, season 2, episode 6. Sundance Channel/YouTube. November 30, 2006. https://www.youtube.com/watch?v=3xEu8MAgOgM.

Bailey, Moya. *Misogynoir Transformed: Black Women's Digital Resistance*. New York: NYU Press, 2021.

Ballard, Jacoby. *A Queer Dharma: Yoga and Meditations for Liberation*. Berkeley, CA: North Atlantic Books, 2021.

Bernal, Dolores Delgado, C. Alejandra Elenes, Francisca E. Godinez, and Sofia Villenas, eds. *Chicana/Latina Education in Everyday Life: Feminista Perspectives on Pedagogy and Epistemology*. Albany, NY: SUNY Press, 2006.

Birdsong, Mia. *How We Show Up: Reclaiming Family, Friendship, and Community*. Boston: Hachette, 2020.

Boal, Augusto. *Theatre of the Oppressed*. New York: Theatre Communication Group, 1985.

Bodhi, Bhikkhu. "SN 46.54." In *The Connected Discourses of the Buddha*. Boston: Wisdom Publications, 2000.

Boggs, Grace Lee, and James Boggs. *Revolution and Evolution in the Twentieth Century*. New York: Monthly Review Press, 1974.

Boggs, Grace Lee, with Scott Kurashige. *The Next American Revolution: Sustainable Activism for the Twenty-First Century*. Oakland, CA: University of California Press, 2012.

Boston Women's Health Collective. *Our Bodies, Ourselves*, 1st ed. Boston, 1971.

Bridgforth, Sharon, and Daniel Alexander Jones. *All These Things: A Conversation*. New York: 53rd State Press, 2023.

British Museum. "The Domesticated Horse in Northern African Rock Art." African Rock Art Image Project. Accessed October 3, 2023. https://africanrockart.britishmuseum.org/thematic/the-domesticated-horse.

brown, adrienne maree. *Emergent Strategy: Shaping Change, Changing Worlds*. Chico, CA: AK Press, 2017.

———. "Murmurations: Grow the Chorus." *YES!* December 28, 2022. https://www.yesmagazine.org/opinion/2022/12/28/murmurations-forward-reflection.

———. "Murmurations: Love Looks Like Accountability." *YES!* July 25, 2022. https://www.yesmagazine.org/opinion/2022/07/25/love-accountability -adrienne-maree-brown.

———. *We Will Not Cancel Us: And Other Dreams of Transformative Justice*. Chico, CA: AK Press, 2022.

Brown, Brene. *Dare to Lead: Brave Work. Tough Conversations. Whole Hearts*. New York: Random House, 2018.

Caldwell, Christine. "Body Identity Development: Who We Are and Who We Become." In *Oppression and the Body: Roots, Resistance, and Resolutions*, edited by Christine Caldwell and Lucia Bennett Leighton, 31–50. Berkeley, CA: North Atlantic Books, 2018.

Cenat, Jude Mary. "Complex Racial Trauma: Evidence, Theory, Assessment, and Treatment." *Perspectives on Psychological Science* 18, no. 3 (October 2022): 675–87. https://doi.org/10.1177/17456916221120428.

Clark, VèVè A. "Developing Diaspora Literacy and Marasa Consciousness." *Theatre Survey* 50, no. 1 (May 2009): 9–18. https://doi.org/10.1017/S0040557409000039.

Comas-Díaz, Lillian, Gordon Nagayama Hall, and Helen A. Neville. "Racial Trauma: Theory, Research, and Healing: Introduction to the Special Issue." *American Psychologist* 74, no. 1 (2019): 1–5. https://psycnet.apa.org/fulltext/2019-01033-001.pdf.

Combahee River Collective. *The Combahee River Collective Statement: Black Feminist Organizing in the Seventies and Eighties*, 1st ed. Albany, NY: Kitchen Table: Women of Color Press, 1986.

Cook, Nahshon. *Being with Horses*. Parker, CO: Nova's Books, 2021.

———. (Nahshon Cook Horsemanship). "This morning, while cleaning stalls, I thought about a person always wanting more from the horse than they already have, and how that makes the horse's life . . ." (Facebook post). March 7, 2023. https://www.facebook.com/NahshonCookHorsemanship /posts/pfbid0ddAKUu9QDfxkyxqb8Mt8EXYdR7nQT4kz4r1sTQygmn Ecb9sfbr33N1RU2hCqHaNMl.

Cullors, Patrisse. *An Abolitionist's Handbook: 12 Steps to Changing Yourself and the World*. New York: St. Martin's Press, 2022.

Dana, Deb, and Stephen Porges. *The Polyvagal Theory in Therapy: Engaging the Rhythm of Regulation*. New York: W. W. Norton, 2018.

Dastagir, Alia E. "If You Keep Putting Work before Health and Happiness, You May Be Suffering from Internalized Capitalism." *USA Today*. June 17, 2021. https://www.usatoday.com/story/life/health-wellness/2021/06/17/internalized -capitalism-harms-mental-health-productivity/7723416002/.

Davis, Fania E. *The Little Book of Race and Restorative Justice: Black Lives, Healing, and US Social Transformation*. Brattleboro, VT: Good Books, 2019.

Davis, Julia Rhodes, and Sara King. "Living Agreements: Creating the Conditions for our Co-Liberation." *Medium*. April 1, 2022. https://medium.com /@mobiusorg/living-agreements-creating-the-conditions-for-our-co-liberation -8acba1dea439.

Education for Liberation Network and Critical Resistance Editorial Collective. *Lessons in Liberation: An Abolitionist Toolkit for Educators*. Chico, CA: AK Press, 2021.

Engler, Mark, and Ai-jen Poo. "Ai-jen Poo: Organizing Labor—With Love." *YES!* July 29, 2011. http://www.yesmagazine.org/issues/the-yes-breakthrough-15 /ai-jen-poo-organizing-labor-with-love.

Eydland, Celia. "Healing Ways Proves Restoration Comes in Multiple Forms." *The Student Life*. Pomona College. April 8, 2016. https://tsl.news/life -style5762/.

Freire, Paulo. *Pedagogy of the Oppressed*. 30th Anniversary Edition. Translated by Myra Bergman Ramos. New York: Continuum, 2000.

Garza, Alicia. "Building Power with Alicia Garza." *Finding Our Way* (podcast). Produced by Prentis Hemphill. August 29, 2022. https://www.findingourway podcast.com/individual-episodes/s3e6.

Gerber, Michael E. *The E-Myth Revisited: Why Most Small Businesses Don't Work and What to Do About It*, 2nd ed. New York: Harper Business, 2004.

Ginwright, Shawn. *The Four Pivots: Reimagining Justice, Reimagining Ourselves*. Berkeley, CA: North Atlantic Books, 2022.

———. "The Future of Healing: Shifting from Trauma Informed Care to Healing Centered Engagement." *Medium.* May 31, 2018. https://ginwright.medium .com/the-future-of-healing-shifting-from-trauma-informed-care-to-healing -centered-engagement-634f557ce69c.

———. *Hope and Healing in Urban Education: How Urban Activists and Teachers Are Reclaiming Matters of the Heart.* New York: Routledge, 2016.

Goodridge, Leah. "Professionalism as a Racial Construct." *UCLA Law Review,* UCLA School of Law. March 29, 2022. https://www.uclalawreview.org/ professionalism-as-a-racial-construct/.

Haga, Kazu. *Healing Resistance: A Radically Different Response to Harm.* Berkeley, CA: Parallax Press, 2020.

Haines, Staci K. *The Politics of Trauma: Somatics, Healing, and Social Justice.* Berkeley, CA: North Atlantic Books, 2019.

Hammonds, Evelynn. "Black (W)holes and the Geometry of Black Female Sexuality." *differences: A Journal of Feminist Cultural Studies* 6, no. 2–3 (July 1994): 126–45. https://doi.org/10.1215/10407391-6-2-3-126.

Hạnh, Thích Nhất. *Being Peace.* Berkeley, CA: Parallax Press, 1987.

———. *Fear: Essential Wisdom for Getting Through the Storm.* New York: HarperOne, 2012.

Harro, Bobbie. "The Cycle of Socialization." In *Readings for Diversity and Social Justice,* 4th ed., edited by Maurianne Adams et al. New York: Routledge, 2018.

Healing Ways: Decolonizing Our Minds, Our Bodies, Ourselves (symposia). Pomona College and The Claremont Colleges Consortium. Claremont, CA. April 3–9, 2016. https://www.facebook.com/events/1648194322134739.

Hemphill, Prentis. "Boundaries Can Be Love." In *Holding Change: The Way of Emergent Strategy Facilitation and Mediation,* edited by adrienne maree brown. Chico, CA: AK Press, 2021.

Hersey, Tricia. *Rest Is Resistance: A Manifesto.* Boston: Hachette Book Group, 2022.

hooks, bell. *All about Love: New Visions.* New York: William Morrow, 2000.

———. *Sisters of the Yam: Black Women and Self-Recovery.* New York: Routledge, 2015.

———. *Teaching to Transgress: Education as the Practice of Freedom.* New York: Routledge, 1994.

Hubl, Thomas. *Healing Collective Trauma: A Process for Integrating Our Intergenerational and Cultural Wounds.* Boulder, CO: Sounds True, 2020.

James, Taj. "My learning and understanding about power and transformation continue to deepen . . ." (Facebook post). July 30, 2020. https://www .facebook.com/taj.james/posts/pfbid02eb5i6jdFsAy2dZyDFKJc7WKLx 67guL7dpQTxY1Mw3HtXGpZkG8mkXPK9dtnY4ioNl.

———. "Releasing the Lie of Separation, Supremacy, Scarcity, Singularity" (Facebook post). September 27, 2022. https://www.facebook.com/TajRJames /posts/pfbid0AgSDmSDSR4TGNnV7jV46Z4HMR9FAFztoK16Dc7xXuy Sn8nTK6AjRhs6GECJiyxayl.

———. "There is Valley Work and there is Mountain Work" (Facebook post). September 3, 2022. https://facebook.com/TajRJames/posts/pfbid0kTCZ R9UzqfdqT2hBfqwHNFffD1Wx7W3EtB3H4XyaoiRzkTUsCmVWXpUDCH nhYbyl.

———. "What Is Killing Us?" (Facebook post). August 10, 2019. https://www .facebook.com/taj.james/posts/pfbid02MELaiXTQo7oNwaqsf3zBymj 5Jhy3VirGa63rPW2P4VxNaocbpXKbzHaQN5Vc9vDcl.

James, Taj, Neelam Pathikonda, Brenda Salgado, and Kristen Zimmerman. *Out of the Spiritual Closet: Organizers Transforming the Practice of Social Justice*. Oakland, CA: Movement Strategy Center, 2010.

Johnson, Michelle Cassandra. *We Heal Together: Rituals and Practices for Building Community and Connection*. Boulder, CO: Shambhala Publications, 2023.

Johnson, Rae. *Embodied Social Justice*. New York: Routledge, 2017.

Johnson, Trasi. "A Spell of Finding." In *Testimony: Young African Americans on Self-Discovery and Black Identity*, edited by Natasha Tarpley, 13. Boston: Beacon Press, 1994.

Jones, Robert, and Tema Okun. *Dismantling Racism: A Workbook for Social Change Groups*. ChangeWork, 2001.

Kaba, Mariame. *We Do This 'Til We Free Us: Abolition Organizing and Transforming Justice*. Chicago: Haymarket Books, 2021.

Kaur, Valarie. *See No Stranger: A Memoir and Manifesto of Revolutionary Love*. New York: One World, 2020.

Kelley, Robin D. G. *Freedom Dreams: The Black Radical Imagination*. Boston: Beacon Press, 2022.

Kelly, Kerri. *American Detox: The Myth of Wellness and How We Can Truly Heal*. Berkeley, CA: North Atlantic Books, 2022.

Khouri, Hala. *Peace from Anxiety: Get Grounded, Build Resilience and Stay Connected Amidst the Chaos*. Boulder, CO: Shambhala Publications, 2021.

King, Martin Luther, Jr. "The Other America" (speech). Detroit, MI, March 14, 1968. Gross Pointe Historical Society. https://www.gphistorical.org/mlk /mlkspeech/.

———. "When Peace Becomes Obnoxious" (speech). Louisville, KY, March 29, 1956. King Institute. https://kinginstitute.stanford.edu/king-papers /documents/when-peace-becomes-obnoxious-sermon-delivered -18-march-1956-dexter-avenue.

King, Ruth. *Mindful of Race: Transforming Racism from the Inside Out*. Boulder, CO: Sounds True, 2018.

King, Sara. "The 'Science of Social Justice': An Interdisciplinary Theoretical Framework Grounded in Neuroscience, Education, and Anthropology towards Healing Intergenerational Trauma." *Journal of Contemplative Inquiry* 9, no. 1 (2022).

Lazarus, Emma. "A Quote from Epistle to the Hebrews." *Jewish Women's Archive*. Accessed July 20, 2023. https://jwa.org/media/quote-from-epistle-to-hebrews.

Levine, Peter. *Waking the Tiger: Healing Trauma*. Berkeley, CA: North Atlantic Books, 1997.

Lorde, Audre. *Sister Outsider: Essays and Speeches*. Trumansburg, NY: Crossing Press, 1984.

Magee, Rhonda V. *The Inner Work of Racial Justice: Healing Ourselves and Transforming Our Communities Through Mindfulness*. New York: TarcherPerigee, 2019.

Manuel, Zenju Earthlyn. *The Way of Tenderness: Awakening Through Race, Sexuality, and Gender*. Somerville, MA: Wisdom Publications, 2016.

McLeod, Melvin. "'There's No Place to Go But Up'—bell hooks and Maya Angelou in Conversation." *Lion's Roar*. January 1, 1998. https://www.lionsroar.com/theres-no-place-to-go-but-up/.

Menakem, Resmaa. *My Grandmother's Hands: Racialized Trauma and the Pathway to Mending Our Hearts and Bodies*. Las Vegas: Central Recovery Press, 2017.

Mingus, Mia. "The Four Parts of Accountability and How to Give a Genuine Apology." *Leaving Evidence*. December 18, 2019. https://leavingevidence.wordpress.com/2019/12/18/how-to-give-a-good-apology-part-1-the-four-parts-of-accountability/.

Mitchell, Maurice. "Building Resilient Organizations." *The Forge*. November 29, 2022. https://forgeorganizing.org/article/building-resilient-organizations.

Morrison, Toni. "No Place for Self-Pity, No Room for Fear." *The Nation*. March 23, 2015. https://www.thenation.com/article/archive/no-place-self-pity-no-room-fear/.

Movement Generation Justice and Ecology Project, "Free the Land Capital Campaign," 2022. https://movementgeneration.org/freetheland/.

Movement Strategy Center. *Love with Power: Practicing Transformation for Social Justice*. MSC, 2016. https://movementstrategy.org/resources/love-with-power-practicing-transformation-for-social-justice.

Myhre, Kyle "Guante" Tran. "How to Explain White Supremacy to a White Supremacist." *Not a Lot of Reasons to Sing, but Enough*. March 17, 2016. https://guante.info/2016/03/17/how-to-explain-white-supremacy-to-a-white-supremacist-new-video/.

National Disability Authority. "What Is Universal Design." Centre for Excellence in Universal Design. Accessed September 26, 2023. https://universaldesign.ie /what-is-universal-design/.

Neff, Kristen. *Self-Compassion: The Proven Power of Being Kind to Yourself.* New York: William Morrow, 2011.

Neruda, Pablo. "Keeping Quiet." In *Extravagaria: The Bilingual Edition,* translated by Alastair Reid, 26. New York: Farrar, Straus and Giroux, 2001.

Nolte, Dorothy Law, and Rachel Harris. *Children Learn What They Live: Parenting to Inspire Values.* New York: Workman, 1998.

Okun, Tema. "White Supremacy Culture." *dRworks,* Dismantling Racism. May 2021. https://www.dismantlingracism.org/uploads/4/3/5/7/43579015/okun _-_white_sup_culture.pdf.

On Being Project. "Jennifer Bailey and Lennon Flowers: Cultivating Brave Space." *On Being with Krista Tippett* (podcast). October 17, 2019. https:// onbeing.org/programs/jennifer-bailey-and-lennon-flowers-an-invitation-to -brave-space/.

Ott, John G., et al. *Trauma and Resiliency: A Systems Change Approach.* Los Angeles: First 5 LA, 2017. https://www.first5la.org/files/Trauma.pdf.

Page, Cara. "Reflections from Detroit: Transforming Wellness and Wholeness." Just Healing Resource Site. June 1, 2010. https://justhealing.wordpress.com /2012/06/01/health-is-dignity-and-dignity-is-resistance/.

Page, Cara, and Erica Woodland. *Healing Justice Lineages: Dreaming at the Crossroads of Liberation, Collective Care, and Safety.* Berkeley, CA: North Atlantic Books, 2023.

Penny, Laurie. "Life-Hacks of the Poor and Aimless." *The Baffler,* MIT Press. July 8, 2016. https://thebaffler.com/latest/laurie-penny-self-care.

Peterson, Tessa Hicks. *Liberating the Classroom: Healing and Justice in Higher Education.* Baltimore, MD: Johns Hopkins University Press, 2025.

———. *Student Development and Social Justice: Critical Learning, Radical Healing, and Community Engagement.* New York: Palgrave Macmillian, 2017.

Peterson, Tessa Hicks, Hala Khouri, and Keely Nguyễn. *Practicing Liberation Workbook: Radical Tools for Grassroots Activists, Community Leaders, Teachers, and Caretakers Working toward Social Justice.* Berkeley, CA: North Atlantic Books, 2024.

Peterson, Tessa Hicks, Keely Nguyễn, Claudia Vanessa Reyes, Dalia Paris-Saper, and Therese-Julia Uy. "Know Justice, Know Peace: Reflections from a Community-Based, Action Research Collective." *Theory in Action* 16, no. 3 (July 31, 2023). http://transformativestudies.org/wp-content/uploads /10.3798tia.1937-0237.2312.pdf.

Poo, Ai-jen. "Civil Society in the Age of Incivility." *Stanford Social Innovation Review*. July 24, 2018. https://ssir.org/articles/entry/civil_society_in_the_age_of_incivility.

Poo, Ai-jen, and Harmony Goldberg. "Organizing with Love" (interview). Organizing Upgrade. June 16, 2010. http://transform.transformativechange.org/2010/06/ai-jenpoo/.

Pyles, Loretta. *Healing Justice: Holistic Self-Care for Change Makers*. New York: Oxford University Press, 2018.

Quan, H. L. T. "'It's Hard to Stop Rebels That Time Travel': Democratic Living and the Radical Reimagining of Old Worlds." In *Futures of Black Radicalism*, edited by Gaye Theresa Johnson and Alex Lubin. New York: Verso, 2017.

Quiroz, Julie. *The Practice of Place*. Oakland, CA: Movement Strategy Center, 2017.

Quiroz, Julie, and Kristen Zimmerman. *Leading with 100 Year Vision: Transforming Ourselves, Transforming the Future*. Oakland, CA: Movement Strategy Center, 2020. https://belovedcommunitiesnetwork.org/leading-with-100-year-vision-transforming-ourselves-transforming-the-future/.

———. *Love with Power: Practicing Transformation for Social Justice*. Oakland, CA: Movement Strategy Center, 2016.

Raffo, Susan. "Dealing with the Original Wounds." *Susan Raffo* (blog). October 28, 2017. https://www.susanraffo.com/blog/dealing-with-the-original-wounds.

———. *Liberated to the Bone: Histories. Bodies. Futures*. Chico, CA: AK Press, 2022.

Raworth, Kate. "Three Horizons Framework—A Quick Introduction" (YouTube video). Doughnut Economics Action Lab. August 8, 2018. https://www.youtube.com/watch?v=_5KfRQJqpPU.

Reagon, Bernice Johnson. "Coalition Politics: Turning the Century." In *Home Girls: A Black Feminist Anthology*, edited by Barbara Smith. Latham, NY: Kitchen Table: Women of Color Press, 1983.

Rendón, Laura I. *Sentipensante (Sensing/Thinking) Pedagogy: Educating for Wholeness, Social Justice and Liberation*. Sterling, VA: Stylus Press, 2009.

The Resilience Toolkit Training Alliance. "About the Resilience Toolkit." Accessed October 25, 2023. https://theresiliencetoolkit.co/about/.

Ross, Loretta. "How to Call People In (Instead of Calling Them Out)." *10% Happier* (podcast). Produced by Dan Harris. December 19, 2022. https://www.tenpercent.com/tph/podcast-episode/loretta-ross-316-rerun.

SAMHSA (Substance Abuse and Mental Health Services Administration). *SAMHSA's Concept of Trauma and Guidance for a Trauma-Informed Approach*. HHS Publication No. (SMA) 14-4884. Rockville, MD: Substance Abuse and Mental Health Services Administration, 2014. https://store.samhsa.gov/sites/default/files/d7/priv/sma14-4884.pdf.

Sered, Danielle. "Episode 19: What Justice Could Look Like." *Justice in America* (podcast). March 13, 2019. https://theappeal.org/.

———. "To End Mass Incarceration, We Must Radically Change How We Approach Violence." *Democracy Now!* March 15, 2019. https://www.democracynow.org/2019/3/15/danielle_sered_to_end_mass_incarceration.justice-in-america-episode-19-what-justice-could-look-like/.

Sheeler, Matthew. "Imposter Syndrome Is a Structural Problem—and I'm Sick of It." 34th Street. April 8, 2021. https://www.34st.com/article/2021/04/imposter-syndrome-generational-wealth-low-income-fgli.

Shotwell, Alexis. *Against Purity: Living Ethically in Compromised Times.* Minneapolis: University of Minnesota Press, 2016.

Sins Invalid, organizers. "We Move Together: Disability Justice + Trans Liberation" (event). Oakland, CA. May 11, 2017. https://www.sinsinvalid.org/blog/we-move-together.

Siriwardhana, Eileen. "The Heart Awakened." Access to Insight (BCBS Edition). November 30, 2013. http://www.accesstoinsight.org/lib/authors/siriwardhana/bl093.html.

Somé, Malidoma Patrice. *Ritual: Power, Healing, and Community.* London: Penguin Books, 1997.

Spillers, Hortense J. "Interstices: A Small Drama of Words." In *Black, White, and in Color: Essays on American Literature and Culture, 152–75.* Chicago: University of Chicago Press, 2003.

Sudbury, Julia, and Margo Okazawa-Rey, eds. *Activist Scholarship: Antiracism, Feminism, and Social Change.* Boulder, CO: Paradigm Publishers, 2009.

Syedullah, Jasmine. "What the World Needs Now." In *Radical Dharma: Talking Race, Love, and Liberation,* edited by Rev. angel Kyodo williams, Lama Rod Owens, and Jasmine Syedullah, 181–84. Berkeley, CA: North Atlantic Books, 2016.

Taylor, Sonya Renee. *The Body Is Not an Apology,* 2nd ed. Oakland, CA: Berrett-Koehler, 2021.

Thanissara. *Time to Stand Up: An Engaged Buddhist Manifesto for Our Earth—The Buddha's Life and Message through Feminine Eyes.* Berkeley, CA: North Atlantic Books, 2015.

Thera, Nyanaponika. "Contemplation on the Four Sublime States: 2. Compassion (*karuna*)." Buddhanet: Buddha Dharma Education Association. Accessed October 2, 2023. http://www.buddhanet.net/ss04.htm.

Thiong'o, Ngũgĩ wa. *Decolonizing the Mind: The Politics of Language in African Literature.* Portsmouth, NH: Heinemann Educational, 1986.

Thomas, Valorie. *Healing Ways: Decolonizing Our Minds, Our Bodies, Ourselves—Open to All.* Pomona College and The Claremont Colleges Consortium. April 3–9, 2016. https://www.facebook.com/notes/1654113608093924/.

————, curator/organizer. *Vertigo@Midnight: New Visual AfroFuturisms &* *Speculative Migrations.* Chan Gallery, Pomona College and Clark Humanities Library Gallery, Scripps College, The Claremont Colleges (Spring 2015). https://www.pomona.edu/academics/departments/art/chan-gallery/vertigo -midnight-february-23-march-6-2015.

Venet, Alex Shevrin. *Equity-Centered Trauma-Informed Education: Transforming Classrooms, Shifting Systems.* New York: W. W. Norton, 2021.

Washington, Harriet. *Medical Apartheid: The Dark History of Medical Experi- mentation on Black Americans from Colonial Times to the Present.* New York: Doubleday, 2006.

Washington, James M. ed., *Testament of Hope: The Essential Writings and Speeches of Martin Luther King, Jr.* New York: HarperCollins, 1986.

West, Cornel. "'Justice is what love looks like in public. Tenderness is what love feels like in private.' Askwith Forum" (Facebook video post). Harvard Grad- uate School of Education. October 24, 2017. https://www.facebook.com /HarvardEducation/posts/justice-iswhat-love-looks-like-in-public-tenderness -is-what-love-feels-like-in-/10155292829161387.

West, Xan, et al. "Can Our Movements Be the Healing." *CTZNWELL* (podcast). January 8, 2021. https://www.ctznwell.org/ctznpodcast/can-our-movements -be-healing-xan-west-kazu-haga-lcf8m-carinne-luck.

williams, Rev. angel Kyodo. "The World Is Our Field of Practice." *On Being with Krista Tippett* (podcast). April 19, 2018. https://onbeing.org/programs/angel -kyodo-williams-the-world-is-our-field-of-practice/.

Notes

Foreword

1 King, "When Peace Becomes Obnoxious."
2 Lorde, *Sister Outsider*, 111.
3 Cornel West, "Justice is what love looks like in public."

Introduction

1 brown, *Emergent Strategy*.
2 For example: Davis, *Little Book of Race and Restorative Justice*; hooks, *Teaching to Transgress*; Lorde, *Sister Outsider*; Boggs and Boggs, *Revolution and Evolution*; Sudbury and Okazawa-Rey, *Activist Scholarship*; Bridgforth and Jones, *All These Things*; Bernal et al., *Chicana/Latina Education in Everyday Life*; Alexander et al., *Sing, Whisper, Shout, Pray!*; Kelley, *Freedom Dreams*; and Rendon, *Sentipensante (Sensing/Thinking) Pedagogy*.
3 For example: Page and Woodland, *Healing Justice Lineages*; brown, *Emergent Strategy*; brown, *We Will Not Cancel Us*; Hemphill, "Boundaries Can Be Love"; Taylor, *The Body Is Not an Apology*; Hersey, *Rest Is Resistance*; williams, "The World Is Our Field of Practice"; Kaur, *See No Stranger*; Ginwright, *The Four Pivots*; Ginwright, *Hope and Healing in Urban Education*; King, *Mindful of Race*; Johnson, *We Heal Together*; Menakem, *My Grandmother's Hands*; Cullors, *Abolitionist's Handbook*; Magee, *Inner Work of Racial Justice*; Akomolafe, *These Wilds Beyond Our Fences*; Acosta, *Acosta Institute*; Haines, *The Politics of Trauma*; Haga, *Healing Resistance*; Birdsong, *How We Show Up*; Poo and Goldberg, "Organizing with Love."
4 The roots and lineages of this rapidly growing political framework can be explored and honored by reading Page and Woodland, *Healing Justice Lineages*.
5 Page, "Reflections from Detroit."
6 Quoted in Pyles, *Healing Justice*, xix.
7 Lazarus, "A Quote from Epistle to the Hebrews."

Chapter 1

1 For this chapter, we have adapted some writing we did about this project in another publication. See Peterson et al., "Know Justice, Know Peace."

2 hooks, *All about Love*; Peterson, *Student Development and Social Justice*.

3 Know Justice, Know Peace: A Transformation and Justice Community Collective took place in the Inland region of Southern California, and included as leadership these authors, Hala Khouri and Scarlett Duarte, and as part of the larger collective, forty staff members from the following six partnering organizations: Huerta del Valle, an urban farm and food justice organization; the Inland Coalition for Immigrant Justice, a coalition of more than forty immigrant justice organizations; the Inland Empire Immigrant Youth Collective, an immigrant youth rights community organization; Starting Over, Inc., an organization focused on housing, reentry, political advocacy, and leadership development for formerly incarcerated people and low-income communities; the Youth Mentoring Action Network, a youth-centric, critical mentoring organization; and Warehouse Workers Resource Center, a resource center that tackles the abuses of warehouse and temp agencies. All quotes included in this chapter are derived from the work of this collective; more details about the research we did together are available in Peterson et al, "Know Justice, Know Peace."

4 brown, *Emergent Strategy*; Pyles, *Healing Justice*; Haga, *Healing Resistance*; Johnson, *Embodied Social Justice*; Page and Woodland, *Healing Justice Lineages*; Movement Strategy Center, *Love with Power*; Venet, *Equity-Centered Trauma-Informed Education*; Education for Liberation Network and Critical Resistance Editorial Collective, *Lessons in Liberation*; Brown, *Dare to Lead*; Ginwright, *The Four Pivots*; and Raffo, *Liberated to the Bone*.

5 Original presenters included Tessa Hicks Peterson, Hala Khouri, Scarlett Duarte, Kazu Haga, Jacoby Ballard, Leila McCabe, Kristen Zimmerman, Haize Hawke, Estela Roman, Susy Zepeda, and Nina Watson. Other collaborators who became contributors to this anthology include Leslie Booker, Valorie Thomas, Kerri Kelly, Nkem Ndefo, Sara King, Davion "Zi" Ziere, and Taj James.

6 A deeper exploration of trauma and how it relates to social justice and personal and community change takes place in the next chapter; in addition, many critical texts in this field are worth exploring, such as these: Menakem, *My Grandmother's Hands*; Khouri, *Peace from Anxiety*; Haines, *The Politics of Trauma*; and Hubl, *Healing Collective Trauma*.

7 Khouri, *Peace from Anxiety*.

8 On Being Project, "Cultivating Brave Space."

9 Facilitation guidelines for the community practices listed here, among others, can be found in this anthology's accompanying workbook: Peterson, Khouri, and Nguyễn, *Practicing Liberation Workbook: Radical Tools for Grassroots Activists, Community Leaders, Teachers, and Caretakers Working toward Social Justice*.

10 Some portions of this section have been adapted from Peterson, *Liberating the Classroom: Healing and Justice in Higher Education.*

11 Pyles, *Healing Justice*, 27.

12 This pulls from both original aspects of McKinsey's Three Horizons framework and Raworth, "Three Horizons Framework."

13 The research undergirding these claims is beautifully explored in Hubl, *Healing Collective Trauma.*

14 Ginwright, *The Four Pivots.*

15 Hersey, *Rest Is Resistance.*

16 To explore these values and practices in great depth, see Brown, *Dare to Lead.*

17 Boal, *Theatre of the Oppressed.*

Chapter 2

1 Haga, *Healing Resistance.*

2 Menakem, *My Grandmother's Hands.*

3 Raffo, "Dealing with the Original Wounds."

4 Levine, *Waking the Tiger.*

5 Dastagir, "If You Keep Putting Work before Health and Happiness."

6 The workbook companion to this anthology outlines many of these embodied practices. See Peterson, Khouri, and Nguyễn, *Practicing Liberation Workbook.*

7 Dana and Porges, *The Polyvagal Theory in Therapy*, 1.

8 Ahmed, "Selfcare as Warfare."

9 Ginwright, *Hope and Healing in Urban Education.*

10 Ginwright, "The Future of Healing"; Acosta, *Acosta Institute.*

11 brown, *Emergent Strategy*, 6.

12 Freire, *Pedagogy of the Oppressed.*

13 Universal Design is the "design and composition of an environment so that it can be accessed, understood and used to the greatest extent possible by all people regardless of their age, size, ability or disability." For more, see National Disability Authority, "What Is Universal Design."

Chapter 3

1 SAMHSA, *Concept of Trauma.*

2 SAMHSA, *Concept of Trauma*, 11.

3 *NIMBY* stands for "not in my back yard," a phenomenon that occurs when residents oppose development or certain land use in their neighborhoods. It is most often directed at land use that is intended to benefit poor people and people of color.

4 The Resilience Toolkit Training Alliance, "About."

5 Ott et al., *Trauma and Resiliency*.

Chapter 4

1 Washington, *A Testament of Hope*, 254.

2 Myhre, "How to Explain White Supremacy."

3 Kelly, *American Detox*; Akomolafe, *These Wilds Beyond Our Fences*; and Menakem, *My Grandmother's Hands*.

4 Kelly, *American Detox*, quoting Laurie Penny, "Life-Hacks of the Poor and Aimless," 73.

5 Freire, *Pedagogy of the Oppressed*, 154.

6 Harro, "The Cycle of Socialization," 618.

7 Harro, "The Cycle of Socialization."

8 Caldwell, "Body Identity Development," 43.

9 Caldwell, "Body Identity Development,' 43.

10 Syedullah, "What the World Needs Now," 182.

11 Andreotti, *Hospicing Modernity*, 23.

12 Andreotti, *Hospicing Modernity*, 23.

13 Shotwell, *Against Purity*, 38.

14 Lorde, *Sister Outsider*, 111.

15 brown, "Murmurations: Grow the Chorus."

16 Andreotti, *Hospicing Modernity*.

17 West et al., "Can Our Movements Be the Healing."

18 Kelly, *American Detox*, 153.

19 williams, "The World Is Our Field of Practice."

Chapter 5

1 Johnson, *We Heal Together*.

2 brown, "Love Looks Like Accountability."

3 I call attention here to the work of veteran organizer and teacher Loretta Ross, and in particular to her discussion of this concept in Ross, "How to Call People In."

4 brown, *We Will Not Cancel Us*.

5 Hemphill, "Boundaries Can Be Love," 50.

6 Menakem, *My Grandmother's Hands*, 295.

7 Reagon, "Coalition Politics," 359, 363.

8 Mingus, "The Four Parts of Accountability."

9 Sered, "To End Mass Incarceration."

10 Garza, "Building Power."

11 Sered, "What Justice Could Look Like."

12 brown, "Love Looks Like Accountability."

13 American Civil Liberties Union, "Mapping Attacks on LGBTQ Rights."

14 Garza, "Building Power."

15 King, "The Other America."

16 Garza, "Building Power."

17 brown, "Love Looks Like Accountability."

18 Sins Invalid, "We Move Together."

Chapter 6

1 Mitchell, "Building Resilient Organizations."

2 It is not the point of this chapter to unpack how racist the caste system is, but I do not take lightly the embeddedness of these teachings in that lineage.

3 Morrison, "No Place for Self-Pity."

4 Thera, "Contemplation on the Four Sublime States."

5 Drake, personal communication to author, 2016.

6 McLeod, "'There's No Place to Go But Up.'"

7 Neff, *Self-Compassion.*

8 Mitchell, "Building Resilient Organizations."

9 Angelou, "Dave Chappell + Maya Angelou."

10 Thanissara, *Time to Stand Up,* 118.

11 Bodhi, "SN 46.54."

12 Siriwardhana, "The Heart Awakened."

13 Nolte and Harris, *Children Learn What They Live.*

14 Hạnh, *Being Peace,* 14.

15 This expression, referring to life as the realm of the ten thousand joys and the ten thousand sorrows, is attributed to the fourth-century BCE Taoist sage Chuang Tzu. It refers to the stages of life including birth, aging, illness, death, sorrow, pain, grief, getting what we don't want, not getting what we want, and losing what we cherish.

16 Neruda, "Keeping Quiet."

17 Neruda, "Keeping Quiet."

Chapter 7

1 Dana and Porges, *The Polyvagal Theory in Therapy.*

2 Clark, "Developing Diaspora Literacy."

3 Bailey, *Misogynoir Transformed.*

4   Combahee River Collective, *Combahee River Collective Statement*, 7.

5   Thomas, *Healing Ways*; Thomas, *Vertigo@Midnight*.

6   I intentionally mention both African American and BIPOC here because the politics are not neatly interchangeable due to the prominence and structural force of anti-Blackness in the United States and globally. If the department had developed any foundation for racial diversity before I entered the space, it would not have been wholly structured around whiteness, the white gaze, and the presumed necessity of maintaining white comfort *always already* at the center of every spoken and unspoken dialogue. So, it does have to be both—I entered with full complexity as an African American woman, a Black-Indigenous woman, a BIPOC woman, and more, but I was conditionally accepted with the implicit assumption that I was there to perform liberal, post-racial fantasy, to stand in for all the diversity which had never before disrupted the whiteness of the English department's tenure-track and decision-making faculty. I then experienced being marginalized and silenced for creating "divisiveness" and "bullying" upon voicing my own analysis, holding others accountable, and practicing decolonial pedagogy—all grounded in my professional training, methodological foundations, and scholarship. No Black, Asian, Latine, or Native tenure-track faculty up to that point had been hired when the department was finally confronted by Black student and faculty demands. Maybe it wasn't an evasive refusal to be intentional instead of leaving things to chance. But in any case, I view this situation as silently/passively retaining white normativity in the field of literature and in academia more broadly. As a Black woman, I was in a special category, separate from some BIPOC bodies perceived as being more adjacent to whiteness, with a particular demand on my racial visibility and simultaneous exclusion from full acceptance due to the foundational ways that anti-Blackness structures the entire racial imaginary.

7   brown, *Emergent Strategy*.

8   Goodridge, "Professionalism as a Racial Construct."

9   Jones and Okun, *Dismantling Racism*, 28–35.

10   Okun, "White Supremacy Culture," 1.

11   Okun, "White Supremacy Culture," 1.

12   Hammonds, "Black (W)holes and the Geometry of Black Female Sexuality," 129.

13   Miley, conversation with author, March 7, 2023.

14   Cenat, "Complex Racial Trauma," 1–3.

15   Comas-Diaz, Hall, and Neville, "Racial Trauma," 1.

16   Spillers, "Interstices," 155.

17 Spillers, "Interstices," 155.

18 Even with the "protection" of a full, tenured professorship in a named chair, and after leaving the workplace, public and covert attacks continue; this is the cost of calling for corrections in organizational leadership practices that overlook racism (often masked as settler-colonial benevolence), equity violations, lateral violence, and ableism.

19 Ahmed, *Complaint!*, 1–3.

20 Goodridge, "Professionalism as a Racial Construct."

21 Sheeler, "Imposter Syndrome Is a Structural Problem."

22 hooks, *Sisters of the Yam*, 6–9.

23 Taylor, The Body Is Not an Apology.

24 Washington, *Medical Apartheid*.

25 Quan, "'It's Hard to Stop Rebels That Time Travel,'" 178.

26 Thiong'o, *Decolonizing the Mind; Boston Women's Health Collective, Our Bodies, Ourselves.*

27 Programming included workshops on Ayurvedic and vegan cooking, flower essences, birthing justice, Indigenous water rights, reiki, experimental movement, spoken word, live music, Afro-Cuban drumming, and a lecture on African American textiles as healing art.

28 *Healing Ways: Decolonizing Our Minds, Our Bodies, Ourselves.*

29 Eydland, "Healing Ways."

30 Eydland, "Healing Ways."

31 British Museum, "The Domesticated Horse."

32 Cook, "This morning, while cleaning stalls." See also Cook, *Being with Horses.*

Chapter 8

1 King, "'Science of Social Justice,'" 210–41.

2 King, "'Science of Social Justice.'"

3 Manuel, *Way of Tenderness*, 78.

4 We are using the term white-bodied to refer specifically to people who self-identify as white as a description in part of their social location as it pertains to race. We are using white-bodied and white interchangeably. We recognize and would like to acknowledge that not all people who are labeled "white" as a racial category actually self-identify in this way. Similarly, we are also using the terms Black-identified and Black interchangeably as well, to acknowledge that not all people who are labeled as Black as a racial category self-identify in this way.

5 See Davis and King, "Living Agreements," for the full Living Agreements document.

6 brown, *Emergent Strategy*, 6.

7 Manuel, *Way of Tenderness*, 44.

8 Somé, *Ritual: Power, Healing, and Community*, 52.

9 Gerber, *The E-Myth Revisited*, 6.

10 This is an unpublished work; for further information please contact Mobius Collective: hello@mobi.us.org.

11 King, "'Science of Social Justice.'"

Chapter 9

1 Later in this chapter we will sometimes refer to Beloved Communities Network as "the Network."

2 The writing shared here, curated by Taj James, draws from and remixes stories and collective writing efforts developed by storytellers in the community over many decades. You will find all of these stories in the endnotes and resources listed throughout this chapter.

3 Some of the stories of the beginnings of this collective movement shift are profiled in the following texts: James et al., *Out of the Spiritual Closet* and later Quiroz and Zimmerman, *Love with Power*.

4 To find out more about Parenting for Liberation, visit https://parenting forliberation.org/.

5 Quiroz and Zimmerman, *Leading with 100 Year Vision*, https://beloved communitiesnetwork.org/leading-with-100-year-vision-transforming -ourselves-transforming-the-future/.

6 Poo, "Civil Society in the Age of Incivility."

7 Some of the Network's collective vision was articulated in the 2017 Transitions Labs: *Deep Democracy Rooted in Beloved Community*. From there they continued to evolve through a series of seven-generation vision gatherings organized by Norma Wong and other "Long-Arc Vision and Strategy" convenings. The voices of some of these leaders were gathered in the publication Quiroz and Zimmerman, *Leading with 100 Year Vision*.

8 One of the other significant pathways of practice in transformational movement building has been anchored by the somatics-centered change work described in beloved Staci Haines's brilliant book *The Politics of Trauma*. It is a practice pathway focused on presence and embodiment that has a strong presence within the Beloved Communities Network.

9 Quiroz and Zimmerman, *Leading with 100 Year Vision*, 8.

10 Quiroz and Zimmerman, *Leading with 100 Year Vision*, 6.

11 For more information about the People's Climate Innovation Center, visit
https://www.climateinnovation.net/. To learn more about Facilitating Power,
visit https://sites.google.com/facilitatingpower.com/vision-power-solutions
/home.

12 James, "My learning and understanding about power."

13 Many of those leaders are profiled in Quiroz and Zimmerman, *Love with Power*.

14 Quiroz and Zimmerman, *Leading with 100 Year Vision*, 25.

15 Quiroz and Zimmerman, *Leading with 100 Year Vision*, 27.

16 *The Practice of Place* (see https://belovedcommunitiesnetwork.org/thepractice
-of-place-transitions-lab/: The Network supports a learning and practice
community of leaders working with their communities on land reclamation
and local economic development efforts that are advancing a just transition
from an extractive colonial economy to a regenerative ancestral economy.

17 Movement Generation, "Free the Land Capitali Campaign."

18 For more information about Deep Democracy, see https://iapop.com
/deep-democracy/ and https://www.providenceri.gov/wp-content
/uploads/2017/02/Equity-and-Sustainability-SummaryReport-2-20
-reduced.pdf.

19 James, "Valley Work and Mountain Work."

20 James, "Releasing the Lie of Separation, Supremacy, Scarcity, Singularity"
and "What Is Killing Us?"

21 This chapter draws from collective story and practice developed over the
last twenty-five years. You can find specific project narratives alluded to
throughout this chapter and more detail on how a large, diverse, and growing network of transformational leaders have been coevolving these pathways of change and practice here: https://belovedcommunitiesnetwork
.org/resources/.

22 For more information on this work check out: https://www.fullspectrum
labs.org/.

Index

About the Authors

Jacoby Ballard is a social justice educator and yoga teacher on Shoshone, Ute, Paiute, and Goshute land now known as Salt Lake City, Utah. He leads workshops and trainings around the country on diversity, equity, and inclusion. As a yoga teacher with twenty-four years of experience, he leads workshops, retreats, and segments in teacher trainings; teaches at conferences; and has been an artist-in-residence on dozens of college campuses. In 2008, Jacoby cofounded Third Root Community Health Center in Brooklyn to work at the nexus of healing and social justice. Since 2006, Jacoby has taught Queer and Trans Yoga, a space for queer folks to unfurl and cultivate resilience, for which he received *Yoga Journal*'s Game Changer Award in 2014 and Good Karma Award in 2016. After receiving prenatal yoga training in 2021, Jacoby now offers Queer and Trans Centered Prenatal Yoga online; he also offers LGBTQ inclusion workshops in prenatal yoga teacher trainings so that queer families can be anticipated and supported in their process. Jacoby has taught in schools, hospitals, non-profit and business offices, a maximum-security prison, a recovery center, a cancer center, LGBTQ centers, gyms, a veterans' center, and yoga studios. He is the author of *A Queer Dharma: Yoga and Meditations for Liberation*, released in 2021, a critical love letter to teachings and practitioners of yoga and Buddhism, and he serves on the board of the Buddhist Peace Fellowship. More of his teachings can be found at www.jacobyballard.net.

■ ■ ■

Leslie Booker is the cofounder of Yoga Service Council at Omega Institute and Urban Sangha Project in New York. Bringing her heart, wisdom, and compassion to the intersection of Dharma, yoga, and mindfulness, she shares her offerings as a university lecturer, public speaker, and Buddhist philosophy and meditation teacher. Leslie worked as the director of teacher trainings for Lineage Project where she shared the practices of yoga and mindfulness with incarcerated and system-involved youth for over a decade. She also facilitated a mindfulness and cognitive behavioral therapy intervention with the youth communities on Rikers Island through the Lionheart Foundation and the National Institutes of Health and shared these practices with nonprofits in New York. Leslie is also passionate about supporting frontline communities to thrive in their work and training future leaders through the Peace Corps' Jaffe Fellows and Teaching Residents at Teachers College at Columbia University, as well as the Dalai Lama Fellows. Leslie is a contributor to *Best Practices for Yoga in the Criminal Justice System*, and to scholarship, books, and journals. In 2020 she was a Sojourner Truth Leadership Fellow through Auburn Seminary, and was voted by her peers as one of the twelve powerful women in the mindfulness movement. More of her teachings can be found at www.lesliebooker.com.

■ ■ ■

Kazu Haga is a trainer, advocate, and practitioner of nonviolence, restorative justice, and mindfulness. He works to support healing for individuals, collectives, and societies by combining various organizing and healing modalities, working in prisons and jails, high schools and youth groups, and with activist communities around the country. More of his teachings can be found in his book *Healing Resistance: A Radically Different Response to Harm*.

■ ■ ■

Taj James is a father, poet, practitioner, strategist, designer, and philanthropic and capital advisor. He is the founder and former director of the Movement Strategy Center, curator at Full Spectrum Labs, and principal at Full Spectrum Capital Partners. He is an official dance instructor at the intersection of wild possibility and urgent practicality, where play and unleashed potential find each other. Taj thrives building community around the shared questions that matter most in our lives: How can we build the relationships and express the love needed to transform our world? How do we support leaders and communities to unlock potential and possibility, see the ecosystem and the whole, and design and act in ways that bend the long arc of history toward justice? Working with transformational leaders, small teams, networks, and anchor institutions, Taj enjoys exploring what it means to nurture the community we have and create the community we need. What are our sacred responsibilities as stewards of land, capital, energy, and life to past generations and our children's grandchildren? By living into these questions, Taj works to create space and fertile ground for seeds to be planted and nurtured, for fruit to be harvested, and for us to thrive in the web of our watersheds and relational ecosystems. Taj lives with his family as a guest on unceded Ohlone land, known by many as Oakanda (Oakland), California. He is a proud trickster, undercover mystic, aspiring Ho-Tei, longtime Zen practitioner, a son of a Baptist minister, and a keeper of the Sacred Feminine.

■ ■ ■

Kerri Kelly is the founder of CTZNWELL, a movement that is democratizing well-being for all. A descendant of generations of firemen and first responders, Kerri has dedicated her life to kicking down doors and fighting for justice. She's been teaching yoga for over twenty years and is known for making waves in the wellness industry by challenging norms, disrupting systems, and mobilizing people to act. A community organizer, wellness activist, and author of the book *American Detox: The Myth of Wellness and How We Can Truly Heal*, Kerri is recognized across communities for her inspired work to bridge transformational practice with social justice. She's been instrumental in translating the practices of well-being into social and political action, working in collaboration with community organizers, spiritual leaders, and policy makers to transform systems from the inside out. Learn more about her work at www.americandetox.co and ctznwell.org.

. . .

Hala Khouri, MA, SEP, E-RYT (she/her), is a sought-after speaker and trainer on the topic of trauma-informed care, embodied social justice, trauma-informed education, and resilience. She has been teaching yoga and movement for over twenty-five years and has been doing clinical work and training for fifteen years. Originally from Beirut, Lebanon, Hala has dedicated her life to the study of trauma, justice, and building resilience. She earned her BA in psychology from Columbia University and an MA in both counseling psychology and community psychology from Pacifica Graduate Institute. Hala is also trained in Somatic Experiencing, a body-based psychotherapy that helps resolve trauma and its symptoms. Hala is cofounder of Off the Mat Into the World, a training organization to bridge yoga and activism within a social justice framework. She has repeatedly served as an adjunct professor at Pitzer College. She leads Collective Resilience trauma-informed yoga and somatics trainings nationally. Hala also trains direct service providers and educators to be trauma informed and culturally responsive. She leads a monthly online membership program called Radical Wellbeing, which supports people through embodied practices and community building. She is the author of *Peace from Anxiety: Get Grounded, Build Resilience and Stay Connected Amidst the Chaos.*

. . .

Sará King is a neuroscientist, political and learning scientist, medical anthropologist, social entrepreneur, public speaker, and certified yoga and meditation instructor. She completed her undergraduate studies at Pitzer College, and her MA and PhD at UCLA. She is an internationally recognized thought leader in the interdisciplinary field that examines the role of social justice, art, and mindfulness in neuroscience. Sará specializes in researching and teaching about the relationship between mindfulness, community alternative medicine, and social justice with an emphasis on examining the relationship between individual and collective awareness as it relates to the neuroscience of well-being and the healing of intergenerational trauma. She is currently a post-doctoral fellow in public health at the T. Denny Sanford Institute for Empathy and Compassion in Human Health and Social Justice at UC San Diego. She is also the codirector of Mobius, a home for the development of liberatory technology, and the founder of MindHeart Consulting. Sará is the founder of MindHeart Collective, a contemplative tech company that she founded to develop AI-integrated platforms, applications, and courses grounded in neuroscience, the Science of Social Justice framework, and the Systems-Based Awareness Map (SBAM), a theoretical map of human awareness she developed and launched with the partnership of MoMA NY to explore our capacity to heal intergenerational trauma and promote the well-being of collective nervous systems. In 2021, she was named "One-To-Watch" by *Mindful* magazine, and she made the November 2021 cover of *Yoga Journal* as a "Game Changer" for her work bridging neuroscience, social justice, and contemplative practices. In 2022, Sará was named one of the 10 Powerful Women of the Mindfulness Movement by *Mindful* magazine.

■ ■ ■

Nkem Ndefo is the founder of Lumos Transforms and creator of the Resilience Toolkit, a model that promotes embodied self-awareness and self-regulation in an ecologically sensitive framework and social justice context. She is known for her unique ability to connect with people of all types by holding powerful healing spaces, weaving complex concepts into accessible narratives, and creating synergistic and collaborative learning communities that nourish people's innate capacity for healing, wellness, and connection. Originally licensed as a nurse midwife, Nkem has extensive post-graduate training in complementary health modalities and emotional therapies and has worked in settings ranging from large-volume hospitals to mobile community clinics. She brings an abundance of experience as a clinician, educator, researcher, and community strategist to innovative programs that address trauma and inequity, build resilience, and shape liberatory change for individuals and organizations across sectors, both in her home country (US) and internationally. She regularly provides trauma-informed subject matter expertise to organizations, initiatives, and governmental agencies. Nkem is particularly interested in working alongside people most impacted by violence and marginalization. Most recently, she led a multiyear embodied diversity, equity, inclusion, and antiracism initiative for the Los Angeles County Department of Health Services. Learn more about her at www.lumostransforms.com /team/nkem-ndefo and www.theresiliencetoolkit.co.

. . .

Keely Nguyễn is a communications manager at Partnership for Safety and Justice. She is a first-generation Vietnamese American immigrant who is passionate about uplifting the well-being of communities impacted by structural and direct violence. Keely interned at the Inland Empire Immigrant Youth Collective, an undocumented youth–led grassroots organization in Southern California, and Start:Empowerment, an environmental justice organization in New York City, where she worked on social media campaigns to mobilize communities across multifaceted issues. Keely holds a BA in public health and policy from Pitzer College.

. . .

Dalia Paris-Saper is a white, Jewish, cisgender female with a BA in American studies from Pitzer College. She currently works as an associate at Orr Group. As a white woman, she enters this research with the intention of learning about and becoming proximate to the communities at the forefront of this project. Self-care is instilled in white people—to always feel safe and secure and to have the ability to rest in this world of injustice is a complete function of her whiteness. Dalia did not have to grow up fighting for her right to exist and be safe in this world. She comes into this research with a commitment toward establishing strong communities as a building block for social change, as well as the belief that wellness and healing are not separate from social change work; they are the work.

■ ■ ■

Tessa Hicks Peterson is a scholar-activist, teacher, facilitator, dancer, and mother. Tessa worked for ten years with civil rights, social justice, and youth development community-based organizations in Los Angeles, then joined Pitzer College where, over the last eighteen years, she has taught countless classes and directed four different community centers as assistant vice president of community engagement and professor of urban studies. She has an MA and a PhD in cultural studies from Claremont Graduate University and a BA in psychology and sociology from UC Santa Cruz. She is the author of over a dozen publications, most recently *Student Development and Social Justice: Critical Learning, Radical Healing, and Community Engagement* and the forthcoming book, *Liberating the Classroom: Healing and Justice in Higher Education.* Tessa teaches classes and facilitates training on issues ranging from antibias education and social justice to empowerment through movement, mindfulness, and art. Tessa is a movement baby—born into a household of community organizers, artists, and teachers whose lives were dedicated to the racial, gender, and labor justice movements of the '60s and '70s. She grew up in the eclectic activist community of Venice Beach, California, and now lives with her family in Sierra Madre, among the foothills of Los Angeles (both of which are the original land of the Tongva people). Tessa is blessed to be firmly grounded in embodied spiritual practices, community, and a beautiful family. Her ultimate work in the world is to engage with, teach about, learn from, and better connect healing*arts*education*justice. Learn more at www.tessahickspeterson.com.

■ ■ ■

Claudia Vanessa Reyes is a social justice activist, advocate, fiancée, daughter, granddaughter, friend, scholar, dancer, singer, and musician.

She currently works for Gente Organizada, a community-led nonprofit in Pomona, California, as their finance and special projects administrator. Vanessa also volunteers in their Pomona Rising social action group focusing on decolonizing wellness. Prior to that, she worked for San Bernardino County's Fire Protection District as a geographic information systems (GIS) technician. Vanessa obtained her bachelor's degree from Mount Saint Mary's University in criminology with a minor in GIS. She then attended Claremont Graduate University and obtained her MA in community-engaged education and social change and MS in information systems and technology with a concentration in GIS. Vanessa's goal is to use her knowledge to work with nonprofit organizations, and eventually start one of her own, to merge the worlds between community organizing and spatial data analysis to have a better understanding of how marginalized communities are being discriminately impacted by social and systemic injustice. The goal is to work with those communities, to uplift the voices of youth in those communities, and to use their generational knowledge to create tangible changes in our society and systems to ensure that we are doing more than surviving—to ensure that we are thriving; that we are given proper educational, occupational, housing, and food opportunities; that we are given the proper physical and mental healthcare in a decolonized manner.

■ ■ ■

Valorie Thomas has been a scholar, speaker, activist, workshop facilitator, writer, and meditation practitioner for more than twenty years. Her interdisciplinary scholarship and teaching center Black feminism, decolonial theory, Indigenous spirituality, literature, visual arts, media, liberatory somatics, and embodied social justice. She is from South Central LA, went to public school, and was taught to honor education and collaborative work supporting young people. In grad school at UC Berkeley as a neurodiverse, working-class, single parent and first-generation college student and grad student, Valorie taught in the English, Native American studies, and African American studies departments. She is currently Phebe Estelle Spalding Professor of English and Africana studies at Pomona College, where she has been on the faculty for twenty-three years. She has held chairs in gender and women's studies and American studies and has taught at Claremont Graduate University and the California Institute for Women. Valorie's courses include Healing Narratives, Literature of Incarceration, and Afrofuturisms, and all emphasize social justice and decolonial mindfulness. Her publications include "'A Kind of Restoration': Psychogeographies of Healing in Toni Morrison's *Home*" in *Toni Morrison: Memory and Meaning* (2014) and "Unenslaveable Rapture: Afrxfuturism and Diasporic Vertigo in Beyoncé's Lemonade" (2018). She also organized a biannual student- and community-centered interactive week on decolonial and interdisciplinary healing education and the arts, called Healing Ways: Decolonizing Our Minds, Our Bodies, Ourselves. She is currently working on a manuscript about her theory of cultural and racial vertigo. The 2023 conference Thinking Its Presence: Racial Vertigo, BlackBrown Feelings, and Significantly Problematic Objects was informed by her scholarship. In 2015, Valorie curated the art exhibition and semester symposium Vertigo@Midnight: New Visual AfroFuturisms & Speculative Migrations. More of her teachings can be found at www.valoriethomas.com.

■ ■ ■

Therese Julia Uy is a 1.5 generation Filipina American immigrant. She holds an MA in community-engaged education and social change from Claremont Graduate University and a BA in English from UCLA. What guides her work in this research is kindness, love, and a respect for others. She wishes to conduct herself as an accompanist to the work and the community that these organizations are both a part of and serve. She recognizes her privileges and positionality as a US citizen, her proximity to whiteness, and being a middle-class cisgender woman. Her values are always evolving, but at the core, there is love. There is compassion. There is protectiveness. These do not change. However, the way they present themselves and the way that she conducts herself through these values, she hopes, progresses as she continues to learn through opportunities. Nonetheless, she is grateful to work alongside the organizations and learn from their advocacy and actions.

■ ■ ■

Davion "Zi" Ziere, the codirector and system architect of Mobius, is an artist and composer working with many Grammy-winning and -nominated talents, a world-bridger and serial tech impact entrepreneur recognized by Google, who cultivates visions and systems that value and respect all forms of life. Born in the Chumash lands of Santa Barbara, California, and raised as a global citizen between Oakland, California, Atlanta, Georgia, Jackson, Mississippi, South Africa, and elsewhere, Zi Ziere is a person who focuses on being present and practices holistic embodiment of the world we wish to live in. Zi was the oldest of nine kids and had a range of talents at an early age; he attended Emory University at age sixteen, was recognized by the US Congress, and was a member of California Golden Boys' State, a program in which many bright talents and future presidents often begin learning more about leadership and practicing it in real-time with peers and federal and state officials. Zi would go on to self-produce and release his first album in his dorm room, which landed him major record deal offers, as well as find numerous initiatives seeking to help us align people with pathways that truly enable us to be who we are and do what we love in life. Upon completing college, Zi went on to become a bartender, as well as the #1 North American sales advisor for TESLA. He was then invited to develop training at TESLA and received congratulations from Elon Musk himself at the age of twenty-one. Once he left TESLA, he went on to write Rites of Passage programs for middle schoolers of Atlanta Public Schools, was recognized by the mayor of Atlanta and the state of Georgia for producing substantial economic development for traditionally marginalized communities, successfully generated millions of dollars in revenue for his startups (Culturebase and Origyn), and turned down millions of dollars from investors who were not aligned with his organization's values. He has successfully empowered organizations, artists, students, and many more to be their best self not only when measured by traditional metrics of success, but also in alignment with their values.

About North Atlantic Books

North Atlantic Books (NAB) is an independent, nonprofit publisher committed to a bold exploration of the relationships between mind, body, spirit, and nature. Founded in 1974, NAB aims to nurture a holistic view of the arts, sciences, humanities, and healing. To make a donation or to learn more about our books, authors, events, and newsletter, please visit www.northatlanticbooks.com.